Cheerful Charlie

Cheerful Charlie

A biography of C.P. McGahey

The Essex Player

by Jan Kemp

Statistics: Robert Brooke

Published by Jan Kemp,
PO Box 271, Great Wakering, Essex, SS3 0JU

ISBN 0 9514606 0 9 – Cased edition
ISBN 0 9514606 1 7 – Soft cover edition

Set in Baskerville 11/12 pt by
Fleetlines Ltd, Stock Road, Southend-on-Sea, Essex

Printed and bound by Merlin Colour Printers Ltd,
The Point, Canvey Island, Essex, SS8 7TJ

Contents

List of Illustrations

Photograph Credits

Cover photograph and photographs 2, 4, 5, 6, 9, 10 are by kind
permission of Mike Marshall.

Photograph 1 is by kind permission of Norman Epps.

Photograph 8 acknowledgements to Michael Stones.

The owners of the copyright of photographs 3 and 7 cannot be
traced and, unfortunately, cannot be given due credit.

Preface

The writer is grateful to many people for their co-operation and kindness in the compilation of this book. All have been so generous in their help and time. In particular she would like to thank Rob Brooke, who has not only supplied the excellent facts and figures, but was always on hand to offer much help and guidance; Brian Rowe, for putting the idea into my head; Mike Marshall, who supplied many of the photographs and also much factual detail; Peter Edwards and Essex CCC; T.N. Pearce; Sonny Avery; Roy Sheffield; Alf Gover; Norman Epps, Editor of the Corinthian and Casuals Magazine; Andy Porter; Peter Wynne-Thomas; Charles Sale; Don Watkins; Jack Mendl; John Walker; Stephen Green, at Lord's Library; and R.J. Evans, at Waltham Forest Local History Museum.

I am also indebted to my father, the late Tom Cable, for introducing me to the memory of Charlie McGahey, and to countless others who took the time to send me letters and reminiscences concerning the subject of this work.

Jan Kemp, May 1989

To Chris, for being so patient, and giving me such valued help and support at all times, enabling me to persevere and see this book through to fruition.

An East End Lad

Charles Percy McGahey – Charlie McGahey – entered the world on 12 February 1871. His birthplace was 12 Nelson Street, the family home located near to the Commercial Road in Bethnal Green, an area which is now a mass of multi-storey flats huddled together in urban despair.

Solicitor's son, John McGahey, married shoemaker's daughter, Elizabeth Walker, in 1861, and Charlie was, as far as I can ascertain, the fifth and last child of that union. Ernest Frederick, the first born, arrived in September 1862; Sydney, next, a year later; Florence, two years later; and Alice in 1866.

In Victorian times the village of Bethnal Green was one of the poorest districts in London, and was only famous for crime, dirt and evil smells. People tended to feel sorry for those who lived in London's East End, especially Bethnal Green, and this is summed up by the fact that the annual rent of a Bethnal Green house was £9; in Poplar £40; and in neighbouring Hackney, £30.

The villagers, themselves, felt that the district had a certain amount of romance and charm, which made the dirt and discomfort easier to tolerate. This personality has long since gone, but the music hall atmosphere was then quite apparent. In those days pretty Victorian girls, with their brightly coloured shawls and huge plush hats encased with ostrich feathers, – not bought off the peg but made to measure – decorated the streets, their hats like enormous flowers nodding in the wind.

Victorian society had an obsessive fear of theft. This was even exhibited in an area such as this where the inhabitants' possessions were of little value other than of the sentimental variety. Bars were often placed on ground floor windows as thieves were sometimes on the prowl in the village, and it was made worse by the fact that police were non-existent on the beat until late into the 19th century.

Dickens' novel, *Oliver Twist*, published in 1838, focuses on the villainous population of the time and, like many of his books, was based on an area around the East End of London. Nancy, the young prostitute, Sykes and the diminutive Oliver himself, were all cardboard villains, but so reminiscent of London's criminal fraternity.

Bethnal Green may have been accustomed to robbers and villains, but it was not used to cold-blooded murderers. So the villagers were absolutely horrified when a blood-curdling murder case, probably studied by Dickens, took place there around the middle years of the 19th century.

Three criminals, Williams, Knight and May, thought to be thieves, were involved in the trade of body-snatching. They sold their corpses to local hospitals, notably the London Hospital, close to Charlie's home, and which was renowned for its care of the 'elephant man', a phenomenon of the time.

In fact, when bodies were in short supply they resorted to murder. The team operated from Novia Scotia Gardens, which was also the address of Dickens' character Bill Sykes. Their practice was to kill young orphans because, presumably, they imagined being homeless they would not be missed.

With one of their victims, Carlo Ferrari, they were not so fortunate. He was known to many city dwellers, for people had noticed him begging for pennies with a cage of performing mice on the corner of a street near the Bank of England. On his disappearance people became suspicious. An enquiry was set up, and eventually the white mice were traced to one of the villain's children.

Evidence of other murders was soon found. Cotton stays belonging to poor Fanny Pighorn, a friendless orphan, were found stuffed in the privy of Williams' home, and this was enough to convict the criminals. Later May turned Queen's evidence and was acquitted, but Bishop and Williams were hanged.

The story was told for many years by one to another, probably in 'a whopper', and those who lived in the isolated terraces of Bethnal Green, near Lamb's Fields or Old Forde, lay trembling in their beds whenever they heard the shout of a man or a scream of a woman. Grandfather McGahey may have even played a part in the murder case, although there is no evidence to prove this fact.

A certain stigma was attached to the village after this event, and people, however respectable, were ashamed. Neighbouring Hackney, on the other hand, was quite the reverse. Although much changed now, in Victorian times it was considered a delightfully stylish place to live. A glowing society evolved, which attracted rich city dwellers who found they could build houses, create beautiful gardens, and educate their children, girls as well as boys, in the numerous private schools dotted around the village.

Hackney was a highly respectable village which possibly was the reason why Charlie chose to inform people that he had been born there. The famous Daniel Defoe, who had lived nearby, described the village with more than a touch of pride. 'This town', he wrote, 'is so remarkable for the retreat of wealthy citizens that there is near a hundred coaches kept in it.'

Semi-detached villas expanded towards Clapton, whilst southwards towards Dalston Junction there was a much more traditional form of terraced housing. Charlie would have travelled this way en route to Victoria Park, the area's most distinguished and exceptional place of open-air recreation.

Relatively small in size, Victoria Park was made as varied as possible by James Pennethorne, a pupil of that great designer James Nash. There were two bathing lakes, with plenty of contrast between attempts to perpetuate the much-admired English notion of the wilderness garden with shrubberies and trees, and areas set aside for ornamental flower beds, 'carpet gardening' as it was called.

This was much admired by 'East-Enders', condemned as they were to a daily environment of the higgledy-piggledy and the dingy, and it must have seemed like a world of wonder to the young Charlie McGahey. It was a world away from the crude 'Comic Taverns', that were all so prominent in Bethnal Green; a world away from the ignorant and ill-refined forced to endure such a pitiful existence; and a world away from the smell of alcohol used by so many in that part of the East End to blot out life's monotony, life's waywardness, and its many disappointments.

Charlie would return to an area not near Hackney, but to somewhere slightly to the south-west of where the murders took place. Whitechapel and the Mile End Road were a walk away, and Stepney Green Station, on the Fenchurch Street to Shoeburyness railway line, was only a matter of minutes from his house. It is known that John McGahey was a railway clerk from 1862 onwards, and he was probably employed at Stepney Green, nearby, which was built in 1849 to accommodate the increasing population in urban London.

The building of the Great East India Docks began the expansion and urbanization in the East End of London. Sugar Refineries and Breweries soon sprung-up, and the coming of the railways helped to accentuate the growth even further, aiding mobility.

John McGahey's position as a railway clerk was a much sought after post. He would have commanded a salary good enough to employ a servant, and earnt for himself and his family a place in middle-class society.

According to L. C. B. Seaman, in his book, *Life in Victorian London*, 'One was a member of the middle-classes if one was employed in a clerical capacity in the banks, in the legal and insurance companies, or in one of the offices of the various railway companies.' They belonged to the middle-classes because they were neither trades people nor manual workers, and would have earnt a sum above that of £200 per annum.

This was in an age when the average family doctor earnt £300 a year, though most middle-class people earnt considerably less than that. Junior clerks might expect £80, perhaps rising to nearly £200 eventually; many of them collecting little more than the average artisan. Engine drivers, skilled cabinet makers, and instrument makers demanded around 35 shillings (£1.75p) per week or about £90 a year. This helps to explain why the long streets of small terraced houses in the suburbs could house either lower middle-class or superior working-class families. Respectability was only marginal in some cases.

People would have looked up to John's father in Bethnal Green, and the family tradition of refinement and respectability would have been carried down from one generation to another within the class-ridden traditions of Victorian Society. It would have been instilled in John at an early age that he was a gentle being, destined to receive a good education, and with the invention of Pitman's shorthand, and electric telegraphy in 1837, it seemed inevitable that like many middle-class sons he would find a position in the commercial world.

John McGahey would have been very conscious of his position as one of the 129,271 clerks employed in England and Wales in 1871. He would have certain standards to uphold. Charles Booth explained in his *Late-Victorian Social Survey of London* that 'a clerk lives an entirely different life from an artisan, marries a different kind of wife, has different ideas, different possibilities, and different limitations. It was not only the wearing or not wearing of a white shirt, but of differences which evade every department of life.'

Although John's in-laws, the Walkers, were trades people and probably ill-educated, summed up by the fact that Maria Walker, one of the witnesses at Charlie's parents wedding, signed her name with a cross, Elizabeth would have taken on her husband's ideals and ensured that Charlie was brought up 'every inch the gentleman'.

By the time Charlie was born, Victoria was mid-way through her reign. Bank-holidays were first enjoyed in the year of his birth, 1871, although at this time they only applied to bank employees. In the same year the underground railway's District Line was busy burrowing its way to Mansion House, in the City of London, and the villagers were celebrating the fact that the last great cholera epidemic had occurred five years before. Of the 6,000 deaths caused by the disease, 4,276 were in West Ham and Stratford, very close to home. These villages were served by the East London Water Company which was known to have been supplying unfiltered water.

Charlie's early days would have been filled with lessons, games, walks, meals and talk. It is not known whether he attended one of the many private schools around Hackney, but it is highly unlikely that he received his education from a state school. The Elementary Education Act of 1870 would have provided a very basic education and would have enabled him to sign his name in a church register, but would not have given him a training for the post of Assistant Secretary of Essex CCC.

By the mid 1880s, the family had moved out of their rather seedy surroundings, and had found residence in Forest Gate, East London. At that time the area was considered to be rather 'posh', although an unprecedented growth in the region around West Ham saw the arrival of thousands of terraced houses, some even standing today.

Considered now to be a rather dull and dilapidated place to live with houses in need of desperate repair, Forest Gate was in Charlie's time a rising and populous hamlet of West Ham. It was a station on the Liverpool Street to Colchester line near to the Manor Park and Ilford Cemeteries, and was part of the Great Eastern Railway network. Near the railway was the Eagle and Child tavern, and not far away was the Spotted Dog. Each had tea-gardens and pleasure grounds attached, and both were well-known retreats for East-End revellers.

The area was a part of Epping Forest which was formally opened to the public in May 1882. Never had the Forest witnessed such an event and £6,000 was spent on the occasion. Queen Victoria came to Chingford in a royal coach, and the railway station and waiting-room were garlanded with roses, azaleas, and rhododendrons, festooned to greet the royal guest. Church bells rang out, bands blasted, whilst dignitaries of Essex were much in evidence. At a time when there was not too much to celebrate, this must have been a high-spot for the locals, an event to last them a life-time.

Wanstead Flats, a stone's throw from Stracey Road where Charlie now lived, was a much sought after place for a pleasant recreation on bank holidays. Hobby horses and coconut shies were erected for amusements, and even donkeys were brought along for people to ride.

The flying trapeze was a firm favourite for the Easter Fair. At this event strong-lunged showmen would bellow the claims of their respective side-shows, and aged looking men with cloth caps and sober suits accompanied their gaily dressed ladies, who sometimes would have a gin bottle in hand. Alcohol flowed prolifically in the hostelries of the village and a good time was had by all.

Extra police had to be mustered to man the area at these times, and under-age juveniles were often up before the magistrates in the days before the fair. Rival gangs brought violence and vandalism to the respectable environs of the Forest, and Charlie would have witnessed Whitechapel and Bethnal Green lads in great numbers, assembled to terrorize the neighbourhood.

By the 1890s, the noise of the fair was causing a great hindrance to the inhabitants near Wanstead Flats, and Stracey Road would not have entirely escaped the noise and aggravation.

In 1892, the residents near to the Flats sent a letter to the local authorities asking for the fair to be either curtailed or discontinued. Their prayer was answered. It was agreed in reply to their request that the number of licences for swings, stalls and shows be reduced to fifty, and the site of the fair be as far from the houses as possible. For Charlie it had come too late. He had already left the village to live in nearby Leyton.

Charlie's diversion from vulgarity was probably to be found in boys' adventure stories. Marryat, Ballantyne and Henty had all produced best sellers, but Stevenson capped it all in *Treasure Island*, written in 1883. A mere boy outsmarted the bad adults and saved the good ones, becoming a *Boys Own* hero.

Other heroes could also be found on the sports pages of the newspapers, heroes who he was to one day truly emulate. Newspapers provided information of rival teams and on the progress of the cricket championship, whilst from 1877, when steamships guaranteed a safe passage of 11,000 miles between England and Australia, test matches were recorded between the two countries.

Charlie was fortunate to be born at a time when newspapers were more abundant and cheaper in price. The Times, which cost 7d in 1817, was by 1855, 4d, and in time reduced even further. By the 1860s printing from a continuous roll of paper had become possible, and by the time the Education Act was passed in 1870, the discovery of the chemical pulp process of making paper had cut down its price to a 24th, from 1s 6d (nearly 8p) per lb to a mere 3 farthings.

The young lad could read about the feats of W.G. Grace and take note of the fact that Robert Peel, only 5ft 6ins tall and one of the best bowlers to come from Yorkshire, was born on his birthday in 1857. He would have realized that without the spread of the railways the press would not have such widespread material

7

to publish, and that trainless counties did not participate in the county championship. Railway travel also aided football, making competition more interesting, and Charlie found he could follow many a varied club.

At this early time it would not have seemed conceivable that this youth would ever excel at a leading sport. He was, however, an able cyclist. Ever since the pneumatic tyre was invented in 1888 he had a bicycle, and took part in the annual 'cyclists meet', held in Forest Gate. Cycles would be decorated and ridden in a part torchlight procession through the streets of Forest Gate and beyond, and it seemed Charlie's success in this event would be his only call to fame.

He no doubt took an interest in the affairs of local football clubs, and was aware that Charles Ernest Green had been the leading light in Essex cricket from 1882. But he could have had little idea that he would soon be playing for not only one of these football clubs but several, and that C. E. Green, who was to become President of Essex in the years thereafter, would play such a significant part in his own life, and launch him as one of the hardest hitters of the 'Golden Age'.

2

The Winter Pastime

Amateurs had dominated the soccer scene since before 1863 when the Football Association was formed. They spread the game of football to urban communities in the hope that it would counteract the feared tendency towards physical deterioration.

Working-class teams were the sides the amateurs played against in the early days. These teams were chiefly in the industrial north and midlands. The FA Challenge Cup was started in 1871, the year of Charlie's birth, and the victory of Blackburn Olympic over the Old Etonians in the 1883 Final marked a significant shift. Thereafter the working-class teams came to dominate the game, and increasingly their players became professionals who were paid much more than genuine expenses.

Efforts were made to halt the spread of professionalism, but from 1885 it was reluctantly accepted. Clubs became limited companies, which meant that crowd attendances and takings became all important, and the Football League was started in 1888 to provide a focus for continuous support of local professional sides.

Charlie had never intended to be anything other than an amateur. He would have had the ability to demand good wages because he would have been in great demand by top professional clubs, but it was 'just not done' for a middle-class lad in Victorian England to receive money for a sport he enjoyed.

He learnt the game initially on the damp, vast expanse of land known as Wanstead Flats. It was a short walk from his home, and in the 1880s the location for the young lad to show his excellent prowess as a powerful full-back.

In 1888 he joined the Forest Gate Alliance before graduating to Ilford Park, where he stayed for a couple of seasons. Other

1. *This beautiful photograph of Charlie McGahey
    shows him kitted out for football.*

combinations were soon in eager contention for him, and before long he was assisting Ilford and Clapton.

In 1892 his exceptional ability came to the attention of Millwall. He was asked to represent the team in several London Charity Cup games. The last of these Cup fixtures was the first ever London Charity Cup Final, and Charlie made footballing history by appearing.

In an interview from *English Sports*, a popular magazine of the time, Charlie has this to say about two further matches he played for Millwall in the same season: 'I remember the very good match I had with the Casuals and another with Everton which was a very close finish. The Toffeeites just brought it off by 2 goals to 1 putting on the winning point from a penalty kick.'

On 12 January 1894 Millwall organized a meeting to discuss the possibility of forming a 'Southern League'. The idea had been dropped the season before when the instigator, Woolwich Arsenal, was invited to join the Football League. However, on this occasion a resolution was passed by the clubs represented at the meeting, and after a subsequent meeting with other clubs a final decision was taken to form a Southern League.

The founder members were Chatham – Clapton Orient – Ilford – Luton Town – Millwall Athletic – Reading – Royal Ordnance Factories – 2nd Scots Guards – and Swindon Town in Division 1; Bromley – Chesham – Maidenhead – New Brompton – Old St Stephen's – Sheppey United – and Uxbridge in Division 2. Before the season commenced the 2nd Scots Guards withdrew and were replaced by Southampton St Mary's, now Southampton.

It is difficult to say how many matches Charlie actually played for Millwall during his three seasons on the club's books because the side did not publish a handbook until 1908. There were around forty games a year and it seems Charlie only played in approximately four of these, so he could hardly be classed as a regular player. Despite this he is recorded as saying in *English Sports*: 'I played some of my best games with Millwall.' Perhaps the flat surface of the Isle of Dogs brought back memories of his childhood days on Wanstead Flats.

In March 1894 Charlie decided to part company with Millwall. Football was a serious business for the London club now, and it could only engage totally committed players. A friendly match against London Caledonians appears to have been Charlie's last with the team, but he no doubt watched them with an eager eye.

Professionalism suited Millwall and the team knuckled down well to highly competitive football. The club was unbeaten in its sixteen matches during the first year in the Southern League, and ended up Division 1 Champions.

Millwall was not the only top London club to show an interest in Charlie. On 30 October 1893 Charlie was invited by Woolwich Arsenal to play in a friendly match against Wolverhampton Wanderers. He was the only non-regular member of the team in a match which saw Arsenal secure a victory by 1–0. Charlie was asked to play in a further game the following month, but an injury to his knee prevented him from turning out on the day.

After failing to form a Southern League Arsenal applied to join the 2nd Division of the Football League, then five seasons old, in the close season of 1893. Arsenal was accepted, and was the only team south of Birmingham in the League. Also selected that season were Liverpool, Middlesborough Ironopolis, Newcastle and Rotherham. It was certainly a very brave decision for Arsenal as travelling was long and expensive.

Charlie would have watched the development of Woolwich Arsenal with keen enthusiasm, but it was City Ramblers which had claimed most of his active service, and by 1893 he was captaining the XI. Charlie was quite fatherly in his approach to his young team, and showed a remarkable amount of maturity for a man of only twenty-two.

He speaks of Frank Mordin as 'a good youngster'. Mordin was a very capable goalkeeper and was first tried on Charlie's recommendation. Charlie also mentions another of the lads Ritchie as having few equals for his age. In fact he considered the whole team was working very well together and improving as it went along.

In Charlie's eyes Sam Larkin was an excellent President who was backed-up by an energetic executive. The only problem was the old one, the ground, and for the first two home matches of the 1893 season, 'Ramblers' were homeless. The Woodford venue, found during the season, was not enclosed all the way round the ground, and it was a threat to the financial outlook that the public could obtain a good view of the game at certain points without 'planking the money down at the gates'.

City Ramblers beat both London Welsh (2–0) and St Bartholomew's (3–0) in The London Cup, but as always Charlie only wanted to win fairly and squarely, always acknowledging any form of ill fortune on the part of the opposition. Charlie recalls in *English Sports* that Bart's had 'a suspicion of hard luck in that competition and their defeat came at the second time of asking.' In the first match darkness fell when the medics were leading 2–0.

A fair amount of travelling was necessary as City Ramblers faced sides such as Ilford, Luton Town, 2nd Scots Guards, Wolverton and Hearts, but they were an enthusiastic team, and did not mind where they went to play a game of football.

City Ramblers had a good season in 1894–95. To quote from the *Sportfolio Portraits and Biographies of Heroes and Heroines of Sport and Pastimes*:

> Last year, 1894–95, The City Ramblers had a very good season. McGahey proved a tower of strength for his side, his generalship when hard pressed being superb. He is possessed of a fair amount of speed, a fact which his opponents are generally quickly cognizant. He is also unselfish to a degree.

Charlie had also been a regular player for Middlesex since 1891, and by 1895 was captaining the side. In 1893 London followed suit and asked him to join its XI against the Army. His success in this match led him to be chosen for the London match against Northants and Beds. The game against Queen's Club followed, and from there he did not look back.

An extract from C. W. Alcock and Rowland Hill's book entitled *Famous Footballers*, written around 1896, sums up Charlie's fine ability:

> Selected as one of a London XI against the Army in 1893, McGahey has been a loyal supporter of the London Association and has represented it on some dozen occasions, last year as captain. In addition to 2 London caps and badge, he has the Middlesex cap and badge. A keen sportsman in every way, he is conscientious and a hard worker at football. There are few better backs in the London District, as he is quick, has no lack of resource, and can kick as well as tackle.

The *Sportfolio* informs us of the 1895–96 season:

The 1895 season sees McGahey playing in quite his best style. He has played many good games for his club and was selected to represent Middlesex against Berks and Beds, and London against Suffolk. A draw was registered in the former engagement, and in the latter, the defeat sustained by the Metropolitan team would have been heavier had McGahey not cleared his lines from a dangerous attack on more than one occasion.

Charlie was spoken of as a well-respected footballer not only in soccer interviews but in an article in the then weekly magazine *Cricket*. An edition in June 1896 has this to say about him:

> Mr McGahey is well known in the football world as a powerful and clever full-back, and although he has not yet played for his country there is no reason why he should not do so later, for he improves year by year.

Both Arsenal and Millwall were enjoying professional status and Charlie, still in his mid-20s, was looking for another club to represent.

In November 1895 Tottenham Hotspur invited Charlie to play in a few matches. In those days the club played at Northumberland Park, which was situated behind the Northumberland Park Arms, a public house in Trulock Road. It was not far from White Hart Lane in Tottenham where the side plays today, and only a tram ride away from Leyton where Charlie was resident.

Charlie played in some fifteen matches that season, three matches around the Xmas period. On Xmas Day 1895, he played in a 'Spurs' game against Millwall on Millwall's ground. The away side was defeated by 3–5, and even in the replay, a fortnight later on Spurs ground, Spurs could only manage a 1–1 draw with Millwall. Charlie always rated Millwall a 'crack team', and his opinion had not altered since he left the side.

Spurs had better luck with matches played against the Woolwich Arsenal. In March 1896, Charlie participated in an away game which saw the defeat of the Arsenal by 3–1, whilst in the return match at the end of the season, Spurs won 3–2. Woolwich Arsenal was struggling in the Southern League, and it was not until the turn of the century that the club's luck began to improve.

14

By the close season of 1896 Spurs was elected to the first division of the Southern League. To add to this the side had adopted professionalism. In fact this decision was taken a short while after Charlie started playing for the club. Another outlet for Charlie's talents was fast disappearing and it was becoming more and more difficult for him to 'get a game'.

To make matters worse Charlie's years with City Ramblers were coming to a close. It appears the 1895–96 season was the last before the club was disbanded. He gained a cap and badge this season, but after this year football took a back seat to the summer sport of cricket, which he was beginning to enjoy immensely.

Charlie would still turn out for exhibition matches usually hosted by a notable footballing celebrity of the time, Roston Bourke. Bourke would have had many dealings with Charlie because from 1892 Bourke was a member of the FA committee. He went on to become chairman of Division 2 and was vice-president until 1904.

The 1897–98 season saw Charlie's name in print once again. This time as one of the officers on the Tottenham Hotspur Football Committee. This was the year that the first handbook was issued by the club, and it may have been that Charlie had a hand in helping Ralph Bullock, a fellow committee member, to compile it.

He was not present in the line-up for a friendly fixture with Glossop North End at the start of the season, and it is unlikely that he participated in any further matches during that season. For most of it he was absent in Australia, resting and recovering from the effects of a serious lung disorder which was to periodically affect him for the rest of his life.

During his absence an important decision was taken by the Spurs club which resulted in Charlie's resignation from the committee. The club was converted into a limited company, after a meeting was held at the Red Lion public house on 2 March 1898. According to the prospectus of the new club, Tottenham Hotspur Football and Athletic Company Ltd; the share capital was £8.000, divided into shares of £1 each. The new company agreed to pay the defunct club a sum not exceeding £1,150 for the assets of the club.

Charlie probably kept abreast of affairs during his absence, and must have been interested in the happenings at the club during this time. He would have been saddened by the news that Northumberland Park was closed for a fortnight from 21 February after an incident during a match against Luton, when three of the visiting players were struck by spectators. Soccer violence is not only confined to 20th century soccer. Victorian society also had its rough element. Hooligans of those times would often terrorize innocent citizens on the terraces, but it can be said that it was to a lesser degree.

Also Spurs were again eliminated from the FA Cup by Luton. This time in the 2nd qualifying round having beaten the 2nd Coldsteam Guards in the previous round.

On the brighter side Spurs finished 3rd behind Southampton and Bristol City in the Southern League. Charlie would have been heartened to learn this and he would have been even happier to know that the team ended up runner's up to Luton in the United League. It was in this competition that the then record crowd of 14,000 people assembled at Northumberland Park for the match against Woolwich Arsenal on Good Friday.

Charlie McGahey had definitely not forsaken his old club for good. On 1 October 1898, he turned out against Bolton Wanderers on Northumberland Park in a friendly match. Spurs won 5–2.

He managed to gain a London FA badge in the 1898–99 season, and it was known he was present in the London FA line-up against the Southern League on 20 February 1899 which resulted in a 3–3 draw. After this time, though, most of his football was played with Clapton Football Club.

Clapton Football Club, founded in 1877, had its ground near the Spotted Dog public house in Upton Lane, Forest Gate. It was near to where Charlie lived prior to his move to Leyton in 1892. Charlie had turned out for Clapton in his early days, and now it was a club that he was to return to represent fairly regularly in his last few years in amateur football.

Before the turn of the century the only competitive games for amateur clubs in the south of England were in the various Cup competitions; the majority of other fixtures were friendly games. Charlie was well used to playing in these competitions. His London Charity Cup Final for Millwall in 1892 against the

Crusaders showed he had the capabilities for such events, and he was certainly part of a Clapton team which was to have much success in Cup competitions in the next few seasons.

Apart from the 1898–99 London Charity Cup final victory over Old Carthusians by 2 goals to 1 and the 1899–1900 3–0 success in the final of the same competition over the same club, Clapton invariably met the Old Carthusians at some stage in the competition during their great seven years in the tournament which they won on four occasions. In 1901–02 Shepherd's Bush were beaten in the final by 7–0 and in 1902–03 Clapton defeated the Casuals by 3–1. It was the Casuals who succeeded in 1900–01 by 3–1, in 1903–04 by the same score, and in 1904–05 by 1–0. They prevented Clapton from winning the trophy three years in succession.

The 'Isthmian League' was formed officially on 8 March 1905 and Clapton was instrumental in setting this in motion. They formed a bond with clubs such as London Caledonians, Casuals, Civil Service, Ealing, and Ilford, laying the foundation stone for the friendships which exist today between all the clubs and players associated with the premier Amateur League.

If the players who played at the turn of the century had not been so reliable and so resolute the Clapton Club would not have built-up such a good reputation. Charlie was one such player during those years, and deserved the mention he received in H. Long's book on *Clapton FC's First 50 Years*. Long said of him: 'By consistently clever and sporting football McGahey steadily helped to advance the club along the path to progress.'

Charlie featured in a piece in *Men Famous in Football*, published in 1904. It stated that although he was a 'good back with City Ramblers, Tottenham Hotspur, and latterly with Clapton FC for the last few seasons he has preferred Essex cricket to football.'

Cricket was, by now, the mainstay of his life, and it was imperative to him that he was fully fit before the start of each summer season so he could give his best to his county. After this time it appears he played very little soccer. He was well over thirty years of age and the tuberculosis he suffered in 1901 must have weakened him. The rigours of one and a half hours on the soccer field were probably taking their toll, and he realized he would have to take a background role.

By the turn of the century full-time professional players outnumbered their amateur counterparts by 10–1. Over 1,000,000 spectators were reaching the football terraces every winter Saturday afternoon, and soccer was now fully established as a mass spectator sport. Support was local, consisting mainly of artisans and lower middle-class white-collar workers who now had some money in their pockets and time on their hands to spend it, whilst professional soccer players were now bought and sold regularly on the transfer market.

Professional football was probably tolerated by Charlie and no doubt accepted, but it was far removed from the game he came into ten years before. Spurs, Arsenal and Millwall were competitive and commercial ventures now, and even Clapton was in the process of establishing the Isthmian League.

Charlie maintained links with soccer until his death. In fact he was still taking money on the turnstiles for Leyton FC until his fatal accident. Amateur football had been the game he had always known and loved. It was the only form of football he understood.

He may have preferred cricket to football, but he would have been lost without the winter game to occupy his thoughts during the chilly days. Friendships were there to be had, and Charlie's warm and engaging personality lent its spell to all who knew him. There were few more popular players, few ex-players who lent so much support. His death in January 1935 came as a great shock to the football fraternity. Football had indeed lost a great servant!

3

An Essex Player

It was only Charlie's inquisitive nature that made him want to join one of the five or six cricket matches played simultaneously every week-end on Wanstead Flats in the 1880s. He found batting very difficult then because everything had to be run out, and he would not score more than seven runs by one single hit. In those days he did not like cricket as much as football, but his opinion of the game was to change rapidly as the years progressed.

By 1890 he was playing club cricket for Romford, where he was to stay for a further two years. On 26 May 1892 Charlie played his last game for the club against Leyton at the Leyton ground. He made only 26, but in the circumstances this was a very good score as it was generally remarked that the wicket played badly.

On the following Saturday Charlie turned out for Leyton CC which was to be his home team for the next year. He made a brilliant debut against Honor Oak making 107 not out in 2 hours 25 minutes. Twice he hit the ball clean out of the ground and made 16 boundary hits helping his club to declare on 200, for the loss of only 2 wickets. This was to prove more than a sufficient score, as Honor Oak could only respond with 97.

The Leyton Military Band played sweet music during the game, and Charlie was cheered by opponents and supporters alike as he returned to the pavilion. It must have boosted his confidence immensely and it is not surprising that he admitted years later in *Cricket* that it was from this time that he 'began to do fairly well at the game'.

Leyton CC must have been more than content with its new recruit. For, as well as making a century, Charlie also managed to do quite well with the ball. He took 4 wickets for 10 runs in only 6 overs; two of these were maidens. It prompted *The Leytonstone*

2. McGahey about to take strike.

Express & Independent to say: 'Mr McGahey showed batting and bowling abilities quite above the average.'

He made some magnificent scores for Leyton this season. In July he hit a good 66 against Brixton, and scored 49 against the same team in September, this time on a most difficult wicket.

Charlie's average this season had been 45 and, with Leyton's headquarters so near to the Essex County Ground, it was not long before he gained the approval of the county side.

He was invited to play for Essex in 1893 at a time when the club was still 'second class'. On his county debut against Derby at Leyton he scored a good 37, but was quick to point out in *Cricket* that he was 'very anxious when he took to the field for fear he should make a mess of it.'

He waited and waited, fielding in the deep for Mead and down at fine-leg to save the runs off Kortright. A single ball did not come in his direction, and he recalls: 'It must have been a record. In the second innings it was quite different as I seemed to be running about all over the place. It was such a curious change of events.'

The county must have been happy with the young McGahey as he was picked to play in the next two matches. These games were against Leicestershire and Yorkshire. Unfortunately, he failed completely, and was dropped for the rest of the season.

After this he revealed again in *Cricket*: 'There was much more to county cricket than met the eye. At first sight the Derby match was great fun and the bowling was delightfully easy to read, but in the following two matches the fun had gone out of the game and I found it an uphill struggle.'

This was not to say, though, that Charlie was not making runs in the 1893 season. He took out his bat in a Club and Ground match against Forest Hill and made a hard-hitting 175. Again, for the Second XI, he scored 112 versus an Ingatestone XI and, at the end of the season, he made 146 not out from a total of 226 for North of the Thames' against South of the Thames Licensed Victuallers, at the Oval. He was also credited with a few 80s and 90s.

Charlie was a hard-hitter from the start. Although his prolific run-getting was slow in coming for Essex it was obvious to people such as Charles Green that, sooner or later, he would blossom into a more than useful player.

When the 1894 season began Charlie was determined to do well. In fact he played in nearly all the Essex games but was dropped against Yorkshire and Oxford University. This was decidedly bad luck for him because these two matches were played on hard wickets whereas, previously, he had played on nothing but dead ones.

He was, however, chosen to play against Hampshire. In the first innings Charlie made only 10 runs, but in the second he scored his first century for the county. A total of 256 was needed by Essex for victory but, unfortunately, they missed their target by 9 runs.

He also played his first county match at the Oval against Surrey this season, and witnessed Tom Richardson taking all 10 wickets against Essex. The lad from Leyton was dazzled by the way Richardson organized his pace, and thought it would be very interesting in practice but too much of a good thing to face in an actual contest. He bowled Charlie with a ball which pitched a little off the off-stump and hit the leg-stump. Charlie was much impressed. Brockwell made a century in this match and, as usual with Surrey, the score was excessive.

Charlie knew he had a great deal to learn, and that this could only be achieved by experience. It took him some time to get out of some very bad habits. He admitted he was 'stumped time-after-time hitting at the wrong ball', and as he notes in *Cricket*:

> One has to play a different game in first class cricket from what one does in club cricket. In club cricket you may take liberties which escape punishment, but the least mistake or error of judgement is generally fatal in the first-class game. Fortunately, for me, there are also mistakes made in the field.

Charlie really began to enjoy the game now, and when he returned to Essex cricket in the spring of 1895 he must have hoped he would secure a regular first-team place.

In fact this season proved more successful than the previous one. He batted in 31 first-class innings with 3 not outs and 702 runs to his name. Charlie's average was over 25; more than twice that of the previous season, but, more important still, he made his highest score to date in county cricket. In his own reminiscences Charlie relates, again in *Cricket*:

> My highest score in 1895 was 147 against Somerset at Taunton, but you will remember that our total was 692. I well remember Carpenter being missed by Tyler when he had made 30, and then making 18 and 16 off his next 2 overs. Few bowlers can have had a more painful experience.

Carpenter scored 153, Alfred Lucas, 135, and Russell 99 in this match in which eight bowlers were used by Somerset. It can naturally be concluded that the Somerset field at times became a little slack.

The young McGahey was also meeting the cream of English cricket, and learning a little in return. Bobby Peel, spearhead of Yorkshire's challenge to Surrey's dominance in the mid-1890s, was the bowler who most worried Charlie in those early days. Charlie said of Peel in *Cricket*: 'He has such a curious delivery, and so often deceives you in the length and flight of the ball.'

He found in the match against Yorkshire, early in the season, that he was gradually being drawn out by Peel. He was playing ball after ball pretty easily but, just when Peel had gained his confidence, Charlie found that he was stretching forward too far, overbalancing, and, consequently, being stumped. Afterwards, he could see he was being lured into a trap, but it was difficult for him to see this at the time.

The return match with Yorkshire was awaited by Charlie with eager anticipation. It took place at the spa town of Harrogate and, as it happened, Charlie found that he was more at home with the Yorkshire professional than he would have imagined. On a dead wicket the ball turned slowly and, in good light, Charlie, ever the acute observer, noted that Peel was able to 'get a lot of work on'.

Although Essex were to win this match they began very badly. Owen, Carpenter and McGahey were all out for 1 run; Charlie was bowled neck 'n' crop for 0. The side went on to score 87, but it looked, at first, on the dead wicket, as if an even lower total was on the cards. Charlie joked in *Cricket* that he was 'getting a good chafing from his team-mates', and that he would probably get a 'pair'. He went on to say: 'If I hadn't to make a 4 or a 2, I would probably have got the spectacles.'

In the second innings Charlie made 55, the hardest-hitting innings of his career so far. The boundary was very short, which made hitting much easier, and he managed to get the ball over the ropes four or five times. The wicket was not conducive to orthodox cricket; hitting out was the only method of play. This was the cricket Charlie enjoyed the most, even if it was more by luck than judgement that he scored runs.

Charlie was not the only Essex player to make a few runs. Johnston scored well and even managed to hit a ball clean out of the ground. The Yorkshire side were left with 136 to find in the final innings and, with Mead taking 5, Kortright 3 and Pickett 2 wickets, it did not take the Essex side long to secure a win.

Charlie would not forget this match for another reason. He caught Brown down at mid-off and, in making the catch, had to fall down at full-length. The result was that he was covered from top-to-toe in mud.

Poor Charlie, so dapper and smart of appearance, felt the eyes of all Harrogate upon him. He remarked later that he had never been so embarrassed in all his life. The physical pains of the game were catching up with him, and he was learning to take the sweet with the sour.

Charlie would have greeted the new cricket season with great delight! It must have seemed an eternity since the last season burnt itself out in the previous August. Although it was heralded in the country's press for many weeks prior to the commencement, Charlie would have to wait until around 1 May, the time fixed by the authorities at Lord's, before he could wield a bat once again.

He was master of his own destiny in his early years with Essex CCC. He was building up his reputation. Would he be able to make a mark on English cricket? Or would he fade into obscurity? These questions must have crossed his mind as he set to work to improve his skills as a player.

He was a product of the 1890s; the age when cricket's modern scope, discovered by Grace, still had much to be explored. The cut, the drive, and the new-fangled spin were all toys to be dallied with, and the buoyant Charlie would not be stalled by such delights!

One had to have a great deal of stamina to stay the pace. It was not for the faint-hearted. But Charlie was not a faint-hearted man.

He was a Victorian cricketer who gave one the impression of being rather heroic. Perhaps it was because he was often seen bestowed with moustache and whiskers, in his early days, giving him a rather masculine appearance. It was the age of open-air discovery; of masculine nonchalance; and the hero would risk absurdity with often no sense of self-consciousness.

This accounted for his self-confidence and his ability to risk vulnerability and criticism. He set out on his task in life with a great deal of optimism, and already enjoyed the excitement and glamour a cricketer's life entailed. He loved the nomadic existence. His life was fired with change. He must have realized around this time that Essex CCC were deemed for 'better things', and that his standard of cricket would have to improve if he was going to help them to compete.

Essex had been striving for first-class status for some time and moved away from Brentwood to their new home at Leyton with this view in mind. Leyton was a heavily populated area, and the ground was part of the Lyttelton estate. The Essex club bought 'the pearl' for £12,000 in 1886, and it remained the county's headquarters for nearly fifty years. In 1890, Dr Grace came to Essex with a MCC side, heightening the club's credibility and, two years later, fixtures were arranged with Surrey, Yorkshire, Hampshire, Warwickshire and Leicester.

Essex CCC then had 825 gentlemen and 81 lady members, and were ready for acceptance into the first-class county championship. In 1895 the time had arrived. Essex along with Warwickshire, Hampshire, and Leicester were introduced into the championship, whilst Derbyshire also returned to the fold. The official elevation of the five counties led to the replacement of the 'Second Class' counties competition by the Minor Counties competition which still exists today.

The club had been building up its side over the past few years for just this moment. The team was led in 1895 by Hugh Owen, a heavily built man, who helped Charles Green arrange sides in the 1880s. He was a dependable bat who became a respected leader, as befitting the son of a vicar.

Alfred Lucas was the veteran of the side. He had played for Surrey and Middlesex before joining Essex, and had been a member of the England team defeated by Australia at the Oval in

3. *An Essex team photograph taken around the turn of the century.*

P. Perrin   Rev. F. H. Gillingham   Russell (E.)   J. Armour (Scorer)   Carpenter   Sewell   Buckenham
Reeves   F. L. Lane (Captain)   G. Tosetti   C. McGahey
J. W. H. T. Douglas

1882, when Spofforth took 14 wickets. Then there was the ferocious, Charles Kortright, reputed by many to be the fastest bowler ever produced, and Walter Mead, known as the 'little treasure', who bowled slow to medium. Both players began their careers in 1894.

Charlie was improving month-by-month, and he did not let the side down. By 1895 he was quoted in newspaper reports as being 'a useful addition' to the Essex side, and was well on his way to becoming a first-rate batsman.

The first season in the county championship saw Essex win five matches, lose seven and draw four. Carpenter made 932 runs in the county championship this season at an average of 31, whilst Lucas was back to his old form after resigning the captaincy the previous season.

By 1896, the county had improved somewhat. After finishing in eighth position the year before, they were now in fifth spot. Essex only played twelve matches this season compared with sixteen in 1895, but they lost only four games, winning five, and drawing three.

By this time *Cricket* regarded Charlie as 'one of the best bats in the Essex side'. He was regarded as a 'great favourite with the crowds', and 'would entertain folk to the full, ensuring that they always, or nearly always, got their monies worth when they came to watch him perform.'

6ft 2ins tall, and powerfully built, his presence was impressive. He would make most of his runs by drives and pulls and would be at home in today's 'one day game'.

He did not blossom into a great cricketer all at once – few big-hitters ever do. Even his failures, though, showed that he was going to be a useful player before very long. He had gone through the usual experiences of trying to play a steady game, with mixed success, but he was meant by nature to be a hitter, and it was thought probable that as a hitter he would remain.

1896 was a very significant season for Charlie – for two reasons. Firstly, this was the first year that he received any real coaching. He told *Cricket*:

> I never had any coaching until this year when C.E. Green sent Abel and Maurice Read to coach us at Leyton. It seemed very funny at first to be told that you mustn't

do this and you mustn't do that. But it was, nevertheless, obvious that the advice was good and sound. If the coaching did not do me any good it was not the fault of Abel and Read, for they both gave the best possible advice. But I am afraid I have got faults which cannot be eradicated – at any rate, by advice. It seems to me that one has to learn by bitter experience that certain strokes are bad – you may be told they are bad, but until you have had practical experiences of their futility, you continue to make them. It is curious that it should be so, but I know it is the case with me – perhaps it is not with others.

Secondly, Percy Perrin came to Essex. Percy, commonly known as Peter, bounced on to the scene straight from club cricket at Tottenham. He had been making overtures in the local press for quite a few seasons now, and he was just the natural partner Charlie was looking for.

No young player could have had it harder in his first match. Against Surrey he had to face Tom Richardson, then at his deadliest best, as well as Bill Lockwood, the ex-Notts player, and Tom Hayward, strangely enough, top of the bowling averages. Surrey had won the title seven times outright between 1887-1895, and they were still a formidable force. Perrin showed no nerves whatsoever. He batted with supreme confidence, not overawed by such great men at all. He made 52, driving the fast bowlers with exceptional power.

Later in the season he scored his first century for Essex against Warwickshire, making 139 at the Edgbaston ground, and finished the season second in his county's batting averages. It goes without saying that the young Perrin made an immediate impression in this his first season.

A more polished player than Charlie, he was, like Charlie, tall and burly, and also an amateur. From a distance they would be mistaken for one another, and it was not too long before the pair were given the label 'The Essex Twins'. Percy Perrin described in *Wisden* how the pair obtained the nickname:

> We were dubbed the Essex Twins by Joe Armour, the Essex scorer for 44 years – a living volume of Essex cricket history. When I started, Joe Armour, in his quaint way, complained that he could not distinguish one from the other. McGahey's

height was 6ft 2ins and mine 6ft 3ins. He suggested that one
of the twins should wear a scarf round his waist so that he
could get the runs down to the right man.

As for Charlie, he did not have a bad season. He failed to make a
century, but he did make 693 runs for the county. He made 76 and
69 against Derby in both fixtures, and his highest score was a fine
knock of 97 against Leicestershire.

On 1 May 1897, *Leytonstone Express & Independent* was eager to
publish some very pleasant news concerning Essex:

> Thanks to the creditable performances of our team last
> season, which resulted in Essex being 5th in the first-class
> county averages, we shall be able to see some fine first-class
> fixtures on the county ground this coming season. Two 'new
> meets' will take place with Sussex and Lancashire, and Essex
> will also go to Lord's for a MCC & Ground event.

In fact Charlie started the season with a bang. Whether the
coaching he was receiving was beginning to pay off, or whether
the support of Percy Perrin had some effect, one cannot be sure.
But his deeds this coming season were to play a major role in
helping Essex to their best year in eighty-two seasons.

The match with Surrey proved very interesting from Charlie's
point of view, even though the game ended in a draw. It was
certainly a game he would not forget in a hurry.

After Essex won the toss they commenced on a good wicket to
make some runs. When the score was on 30 Carpenter was
dismissed and, 14 runs later, Fane was caught at slip. The twins
then got to work. At lunch, the score was 139, with Perrin on 44
and Charlie on 49. Both batted confidently after lunch, and 42
more were added before Perrin was run out. After 2hrs 10 mins he
went for 63.

When Charlie was on 94 he made one of the biggest mistakes he
was ever to make whilst at the crease. Attempting to take a fine 6
for his century off the 'little Guv'nor', Bobby Abel, he jumped out,
and saw his middle-stump disturbed. Abel was ecstatic. This was
his only wicket in 12 overs, although 4 of these were maidens.

David Kynaston describes the departure in his book, *Bobby
Abel, Professional Batsman*:

> A humiliating dismissal was that of McGahey at the Oval in

4. *A big hit in prospect.*

1897, when on 94, he jumped in to a ball from Abel, and made a wild attempt to hit, only of course to hear, sometime afterwards, the familiar rattle.

The Essex side made 316 in their first innings, whilst Surrey made 199 in their reply. Essex then went on to score 244-8 before declaring. Charlie was probably still smarting from the foolish error he made in the previous innings because, at his second attempt, he could only manage one solitary run. Surrey was then set 362 runs to win. After being 27-3 Surrey looked in trouble, but Abel set about matters and allowed the game to peter out into a draw.

Charlie did not allow his misfortune to cloud his game for long. In different circumstances 94 would not have seemed a bad total on which to start the season. He followed it up with a fine 51 in just over an hour against Warwickshire. Although this was a drawn game it was notable for a good century from Bob Carpenter, and a splendid 120 from W.G. Quaife.

Essex followed this draw by beating Yorkshire at Leyton. It was a disheartening match for Charlie as he could only manage 10 and 16, but Korty was quick to take 5 wickets in the first innings as Yorkshire were skittled out for 154. He added to this success by taking 3 second innings wickets, leaving Essex 132 runs to win. Fine bowling by Hirst left Essex in trouble at 93-7, but then Kortright and Mead came together to see the home side to victory in fine fashion.

Charlie was in the limelight again when his team met Hampshire in the latter part of June. Carpenter and Charlie dismayed the Hampshire bowlers, and a trial of no less than seven were needed. The century went up in the first hour, with Charlie being the first to go with an admirable 53. Essex made a total of 367, which was too much for the opposition who could only manage a score of 280 in their two innings.

When Warwickshire came to Leyton Essex were just recovering from their first defeat by a county that season. Essex had slumped in their match against Lancashire at Old Trafford, although it is said, 'the umpiring left much to be desired'. They were eager for a win at Leyton, and the twins were not to let them down.

In a high scoring match Essex batted the whole of the first day for 393. However, many wickets were down, and on the following day the innings closed for a formidable 489. Perrin made 158 and Charlie, in fine fettle, managed a good 81. This was too much for Warwickshire, who collapsed to an abject innings defeat.

This good win took Essex to fourth in the championship table – a dull draw at Derby, and a thrilling win by one run over Yorkshire at Huddersfield saw them in second place. They had beaten Yorkshire on their home ground, and must have seemed on a crest of a wave.

A few days later Essex travelled down to Hove to play against talented Sussex. Charlie made 140 in this match, and Sussex was forced to follow-on. But in the Sussex second innings Ranji, who made only 7 runs in the first innings, was in fine form. He mustered 170 in less than three hours, saving his side from certain defeat.

Essex then went on to beat Lancashire on home ground. Desperate to turn the tables on the northern side after their unsatisfactory defeat at Old Trafford, Essex made 290 in the first innings, and Charlie was the star with a fine 87. George Bull ensured Lancashire had to follow on by taking 7 wickets, and repeated the performance in the 2nd innings leaving Essex 140 to make to clinch victory.

They were in with a real chance of securing the championship. If Essex could beat Surrey at Leyton the title would be a reality. For a team which had only recently achieved first-class status this must have seemed like a fairy-tale dream. Their success was helped by the fact that nine of the side were under 30 and nine of the side were capable of scoring 50 or more. *The Times* was kind in its overture to Essex saying:

> Essex have risen from mediocrity to greatness in little more than one season, and their success has been almost wholly the work of natural talent developed under the guardianship of that splendid Uppingham & Cambridge bat C.E. Green.

Unfortunately, the win that would have made Essex champions this season did not materialize. The game against Surrey ended in devastating defeat, and the season finished with a drawn game against Hampshire.

In the Surrey game Essex were unlucky in finding Tom

Richardson in superb form. He took 6 wickets whilst Essex struggled to make 143. Abel hit a magnificent 82 to give Surrey a first innings lead of 121. Tom Hayward then found form in Surrey's second innings. He took 6-31 as Essex were skittled out for 130. This time *The Times* was fast to criticize claiming 'Essex failed dismally in this overwhelming defeat'.

Essex eventually finished third in the table, behind Lancashire and Surrey. If only they had snatched victory from one of their 7 drawn games, or had not had such bad luck with the umpiring at Old Trafford, the title would have been in the bag. But they certainly could not complain at the way they played this season. They had beaten Yorkshire twice, and although the margin was slight in each case, it was a magnificent achievement.

Yorkshire was second only to Surrey as the supreme team of the 1890s, and whilst Yorkshire's prizes were bowlers such as Hirst and Rhodes, and the great all-round amateur, F.S. Jackson, the side's batting strength was based on the great opening partnership of Brown and Tunnicliffe.

Charlie had the best season of his career so far. For the first time he had passed the 1,000 run mark in first-class cricket, a feat he was to achieve on nine occasions thereafter. He had played his heart out, and took his cricket very seriously. He knew he had to play well to deserve a place in such a young team and, in fact, found the game a great strain at this stage.

He ended the cricket season physically exhausted. He had never been strong, and had always suffered from a weak chest. Black and bleak conditions in London's East End did not help matters, and the area around Forest Gate had a great reputation for flooding. Bryant & May's match factory was sited by the nearby River Lea, and the river acquired an opaque colour and a 'urinous' smell, which could not have been too healthy for the local inhabitants.

It would have been a terrible shame if a player with so much ability had burnt himself out so early. C.E. Green realized this factor and, according to James Thorpe, the Leyton club cricketer, paid for Charlie to make several trips to Australia during the close season.

Thorpe says of this: 'Although a big, muscular fellow, McGahey was not strong enough to stand the rigours of the English

33

winter, and by the kindness of the late Charles Green, made several visits to Australia to avoid it.'

Sewell also backs up this point: 'McGahey for all his fine physique, did not enjoy good health. He once went for a health voyage on a sailing ship to Australia, during which time, so he told me, one of his chief recreations was making pals with the "rats", on deck, four legged "uns".'

It is probable that Charlie left St Pancras on 17 September with A.E. Stoddart's team of 13. The boat stopped at Port Said and Colombo, and the weather was hot and sultry, but cricket was played at neither place. For England, this was a disappointing tour. Although winning the first Test, they had the misfortune to lose the following four, and there were frequent accounts of players being bitten by mosquitoes. Ted Wainwright, the popular Yorkshire all-rounder, who was eleventh in the team's bowling averages and played in four Tests, none too successfully as a batsman, is reputed to have kissed the ground in relief when he saw his first English cricket pitch on his return to England in 1898.

Having said this, Charlie does not appear to have had a bad visit. He was not under the pressures encountered by the players and, although the journeys were tiresome and the conditions not quite up to English standards, he did not have to worry about hostile crowds, bad umpiring, nor the illnesses and injuries that niggled the touring party.

His *Wisden Obituary* certainly seems to back up the view that Charlie did not have a bad winter. It says: 'More than once indifferent health threatened to cause his premature retirement from cricket, but during a trip to Australia, in the winter of 1897, he threw off the dangers of a break-down.'

The journey to Australia certainly did not sour his thoughts on the game; the journey to Australia certainly did not make him lethargic. He returned from Australia as keen and as full of life as ever, and was ready for all life had in store for him. His batteries were recharged: ready for action; ready for the 1898 cricket season: a season which, like many to come, was to see him making runs, taking wickets, and not too seldom, making headlines.

4

Always a Gentleman

In the cricket world everyone took for granted the social gulf between amateur and professional players. The professional conceded that the amateur was a player, but would not dream of claiming the status for himself: he accepted that his dressing-room was different, and usually inferior to his amateur counterpart; he accepted that he would walk out of a different gate; and that his accommodation, when on tour, had only the bare comforts. He was respectful and subservient, realizing he would never hold a position of social authority.

Amateurs ran cricket. The amateur captain was dutifully addressed by the professionals as 'Sir'. The professional could not venture into the main part of the pavilion, and often had to have a snack at the local pub as the ground would not always provide lunch for such inferior beings.

Joe Darling, the old Australian cricket captain, re-iterates some harsh sentiments felt by the professionals in a book he wrote on his recollections of the game:

> I note that there is a lot of discussion in England about the amateurs and professionals using the same dressing-rooms. In my time the professional cricketers were not treated fairly by the authorities in not allowing them the right to sit at the same dining-tables or use the same dressing-rooms as the amateurs. In my time when playing against 'All England' at Lord's, it was a very common thing for an amateur and a professional to open the innings. The professional had to be waiting at his gate, but dare not go on to the members' pavilion and enter the playing ground first. The amateur and professional then walked to the wickets from different gates, about 50 yards apart, so did not actually meet until they got to the wicket.

David Kynaston, in his book, *Bobby Abel, Professional Batsman*, tells about the wages paid, and the problems encountered by the professional cricketer when his playing days were over:

> An established county professional might hope to clear circa £120-£150 from a season; a player of International standard nearer £200. Such sums were appreciably more than the approximate £95 a year that an unskilled town or agricultural labourer earned, and could even be a little above the annual earnings of most skilled artisans. The problem with being a professional cricketer was not so much that it paid poorly, at least in comparison with the jobs of other working-class men, but that there was little provision, apart from the rather ineffectual Cricketers Fund Friendly Society, for when that very specialized money-making ability came to an end.

Charlie soon realized that this drab existence was not for him. He much preferred the life of gaiety and splendour enjoyed by the 'Gentlemen'. Fortunately the gods were to shine on him. Charles Green, who hailed from neighbouring Walthamstow, noticed Charlie when he was just a rough hitter for his local club side Leyton. His style and panache endeared him to the older man, who recognized that 'a man from such a background would never be classed as a professional, and that his polish and joie de vivre would do much to recommend him to the respectability of the amateur classes.'

One imagined the classic amateur to be a man of wealth, but this was not always the case. Cricketers also managed to play first-class cricket and keep their amateur status by becoming secretaries or treasurers of their county side. They were known as 'paid amateurs' and existed before the 20th century, lasting until the abolition of the amateur status in 1963. Charlie was one such fellow. His numerical ability did not go unnoticed, and, from 1893, he became Assistant Secretary to his county side, a position, according to Tom Pearce, worth around £200 per annum.

Much has been said about the paid amateur, and most of it none too complimentary. This has probably been made worse because W.G. Grace, the most notable amateur of all, greatly abused this privilege. As Joe Darling points out: 'Dr Grace insisted upon, and received, £3,000 before he would come out to Australia with the Earl of Sheffield's team, and also had his expenses paid besides for his wife and daughter.'

In fact, Dr Grace also demanded the cost of a locum whilst he was abroad, as well as a £20 match fee for every match he played for Gloucestershire. By the mid 1890s criticism began to mount about the blatant scale of the doctor's 'shamaterism' and, by the end of the century, the great man's performances were at last waning and he could no longer make his own terms in quite the same way.

Not all amateurs abused the system in this fashion, but many such as Charlie would not have survived financially to keep up a social front if there had not been 'perks'. The Surrey committee soon found that if it treated all the country's amateurs as well-to-do men of leisure there would be few cricketers of any calibre left to meet the Players at the Oval.

David Kynaston points out, again in his book, *Bobby Abel, Professional Batsman*: 'In 1898, Townsend and Sewell each received £4 as expenses for playing in the Oval match, while four years later bats were presented to Beldam, McGahey and W.G. Grace himself for their scores for the gentlemen.'

This seems to contradict an article in *Daily Express*, written by C.B. Fry in 1903, which discusses the controversial question of amateur expenses. He distinguished between the amateur who is a salaried treasurer or secretary, which he quotes as 'a matter of opinion as to its legitimacy', and under-the-counter payments by the club – surreptitious bank-notes found in boots – which he says were a 'journalistic fancy'.

'The usual practice', he asserted, 'was that county clubs, one and all, pay their amateurs out-of-pocket expenses, i.e. hotel bills and railway tickets, and no amateur, however clever he may be at accounts, has yet succeeded in going through a cricket season without being considerably out of pocket at the finish.'

The Gentlemen versus Players matches were important events in the cricketing calendar at the turn of the century. These contests were first played as early as the first decade of the 19th century. By the time Charlie was playing the sides would meet three times a year, at Lord's, the Oval, and at the Scarborough or Folkestone Festivals.

It was in 1865 that W.G. Grace first represented the Gentlemen. This was at the Oval and he was a few days short of his seventeenth birthday. He made 23 and 12 with the bat, and had match figures of 7–125. Quite a feat for a lad so young!

He dominated these fixtures for forty years; when he finally bowed out on 18 July 1906 – his fifty-eighth birthday – he had made eighty appearances.

Charlie could not claim success such as this, but he was good enough to play for the Gentlemen, each time at the Oval, from 1897 to 1903, and again in 1905. Perhaps his selection for only the Oval matches showed that his ability was not tip-top because he was not regarded as amongst the cream of the amateurs who were always selected for the Lord's games.

He appeared with moderate success though, and this is summed up in a piece from an *Essex Year Book*:

> Although never being selected for Gentlemen versus Players at Lord's, McGahey appeared on several occasions in the Oval match, twice with great success. In 1900, the Gentlemen were set 351 to win, and thanks to C.J. Burnup 123 and McGahey 68 they nearly pulled it off, losing by only 37 runs. The second occasion was in 1902 when the Gentlemen went in 148 behind on the first innings and lost 6-96, then McGahey played a superb innings of 65 n.o. he and Jephson putting on 73 and saving the game.

During Charlie's visits to the Oval he would have noticed a change of pavilion. The old decaying structure was swept away in the latter months of 1897, and a new, more elegant, more comfortable building was erected in its place. An article in *The Times*, 30 March 1898, entitled *From the new Pavilion at the Oval* states:

> There has been a transformation at the Oval from the old irregular pavilion to the new palatial structure since Surrey beat Lancashire at the end of August last.
>
> The old pavilion and the old tavern with all their cricket traditions have been swept away and there now stands in their place a handsome red-brick pile of buildings which commands the admiration of all those who pass along the Harley Ford Road to Vauxhall and the West End. The new red-brick building with bath stone facings has a frontage of 300 feet. It much surpasses in its imposing nature its model

the Lancashire pavilion at Old Trafford, Manchester, and
also the handsome red-brick and terra-cotta work at Lord's.

The Players more often than not beat the Gentlemen so Charlie
would not have had too much to be thrilled about. On the other
hand, there was a great deal of prestige attached to these events,
and in fact the prestige was greater than selection for the national
team. Although selection for the MCC was not to be sneezed at, it
did not have the same significance as it does in present times.

Very much a part of the cricket establishment were the various
festivals which were played with much merriment. The Canter-
bury week, held in August, still sees the tradition flourish today.
Its home since 1847 is the St Lawrence Ground with its elegant,
attractive trees and lovely sloping ground; a ground which has
welcomed creamy-coloured tents and cavalier-type characters for
many years in typical fashion. Cricket is played by day and
theatrical entertainment by night much as it was in Charlie's
time.

Scarborough, another venue, was a place where cricket was
played for fun. Dating from 1876 the Scarborough Festival was an
event where large holiday crowds were expected, and was often
the scene of many close finishes. Sixes were the stuff of
Scarborough, breezily placed before the sea, and was traditionally
the scene of the last match played by most of the touring teams.
Theatrical performances were also often linked with the Scarborough Festival.

The southern answer to Scarborough might be Hastings where
the Festival dates back to 1887. The tight, little oblong shaped
ground in the middle of the town has views of the historic castle,
as well as a twang of salty air. Its combination of short boundaries
and seaside spirits has inspired many a display of dazzling hitting.
It is a 'six-hitters' paradise.

This was probably a reason why Charlie loved to play at
Hastings. For a hard-hitting player such as himself a ground such
as this was a place sent from heaven. On 3 September 1907 he
played there for the Gentlemen of the South against the Players
from the same region.

The Gentlemen had secured a 102 lead on the first innings
when they went in again. On 25-3, and Charlie already batting,

Jessop came in to join him. The pair put on 108 for the 4th wicket in 35 minutes. Jessop dominated the partnership, scoring 87 of the runs and reaching 50 in 24 minutes, but Charlie was there in good support and, when Charlie was out on 133–4, the Gentlemen were well on their way to making a respectable total.

Life for the amateur was care-free and a pleasure to savour in the days known as the Golden Age of cricket. Neville Cardus described the time as 'regal and spectacular', and no doubt Charlie would have been the first to echo these sentiments.

His amateur status brought him into the company of the cream of the cricketing establishment at a time when banquets, balls and Edwardian tea-parties were all delights to enjoy. Even if he could not always afford to live the life of splendour he did so when he could, a statement, which, according to P. Morrah in his book on the *Golden Age of Cricket*, seems to sum up the amateur gent.

Charlie's connections with the Gentlemen brought him naturally into continued contact with W.G. Grace, and so it was no surprise that WG invited him to play for London County Cricket Club, the club Grace founded in 1899 at Crystal Palace.

The idea was that WG would help promote the Crystal Palace as a tourist haunt, for it was thought that thousands of folk would flock to view him at the wicket, rather as if he were 'a mounted sentry', or a 'Beefeater' at the Tower of London. He was the second best-known Victorian gentleman after Gladstone, and it was thought that his matches would create a great spectacle.

The Crystal Palace was like a kind of gigantic baroque greenhouse, designed by the Duke of Devonshire's head gardener, Joseph Paxton, and erected in Hyde Park to house the great Exhibition of 1851. In 1854 it was re-erected as the centre-piece of a sports and recreational complex at Penge, and until the disastrous fire of 1936, a celebrated landmark.

The establishment was usually benign in its attitude to the ventures of WG, but after a few games in 1899 the MCC recognized many of London County's matches as first-class. The club was set up in the wake of the formation of the London County Council in 1888, and many distinguished players were to represent the club, resplendent in their dark green caps with red and yellow bands.

WG chose as his vice-captain, William Murdoch. Murdoch was

a great friend of Grace, and he was often seen in Grace's company on the golfing links of England. Murdoch was generally regarded as one of the greatest of Australian batsmen, and captained Sussex for six years from 1893.

It was at London County that WG discovered Len Braund, the England and Somerset all-rounder. He went on to make three centuries for County, two more than Ranji, who played only occasionally for the club. In forty-eight innings Braund scored 1,432 runs and took 143 wickets, at a cost of 3,609 runs.

WG loved to have successful players around him – colourful characters who added sparkle to the game. In 1901, the South Africans visited our shores, and some of their players represented County.

At the same time there were successful Englishmen hitting the headlines who Grace was quick to include in his team. This is probably the reason why Charlie fitted the bill so adequately. Grace would have witnessed Charlie's improvement in the game during the late 1890s, and would have been proud to acknowledge him as one of the star players of 1901.

Charlie's first match for London County was against Leicester at Crystal Palace in 1901. Amongst his team-mates in that match were F.L. Fane, Essex captain before Charlie, and Quaife, the Warwickshire professional, who was selected with Charlie the following winter to tour Australia. Murdoch and Grace were also present.

McGahey turned out bowling figures of 4–17 runs off 10 overs in the first innings, but a full flow of runs were not to come until later in the season.

Turning out for London County against Warwickshire at Crystal Palace on 27 August 1901 Charlie made a score which must have contributed considerably to him being one of the five cricketers of the *Wisden Almanack* for that season. He devastated the Warwickshire attack and floored the fielders to make a fine 115. It was apparently quite a spectacle!

Several notabilities were invited to play in this game. Maitland Hathorn, who headed the batting averages for the South Africans, came to London County after scoring 239 against Cambridge University at Fenners, while Jimmy Sinclair, the most successful bowler on the tour, who had taken 61 wickets, also played. Then there was Ernest Halliwell, the Middlesex-born player who in 1901 was living in South Africa, and WG Junior, who sadly was to lose his life from the effects of an appendicitis operation in 1905.

The saddest character to play in this side with Charlie was Bill Brockwell. Brockwell was a fine England and Surrey player who toured South Africa and also Australia with A.E. Stoddart's team of 1894–95. He played in seven Test Matches in England, but on leaving first-class cricket he fell on hard times and died in abject poverty.

In 1902 Charlie McGahey was again invited to turn out for London County, and he joined his twin Percy Perrin in the latter's only game for County. Perrin made 11 and 46 not out, but Charlie played a more significant part in the match.

Leicestershire was the opposition, and both Charlie and Billy Murdoch put on a fine display of batting. Showmen at their best they entertained the crowd to the full allowing them to witness a fine 3rd wicket partnership. The pair added 67 in a couple of hours, Murdoch making 132 and Charlie 75. The scores in this highly entertaining match were Leicestershire 280 and 227–3, County 327 and 86–0, but unfortunately time ran out preventing a County victory.

C.B. LLewelyn, an itinerant South African, also played in this match. He was to play Test cricket for his own country, but played for many years in England. He was born in Pietermaritzburg, South Africa, in 1876, and represented London County in various matches between 1901–03, as well as playing 196 matches for Hampshire between 1899–1920 and participating in the Lancashire League.

His only double-century was 216 for Hampshire versus South Africa at Southampton in 1901, while his best bowling figures were 9–55 for London County versus Cambridge University at Crystal Palace in 1902. He left Hampshire due to a disagreement over terms and, after touring Australia with the 1910–11 South Africans, came back to play league cricket in England. He was co-opted into the South African side in England in 1912, playing in five Tests and one other first-class match.

Charlie was not selected for any matches in 1903, but 1904 saw him return once again to the Crystal Palace. Early in the season he played in a few prominent matches. These were more significant for the players who accompanied him rather than for his own contributions.

A.E. Knight, who had represented England, played in one of the games. He was a notable player for London County during the 1903–04 seasons, and was later well-known for his book, *The Complete Cricketer*. The England and Gloucestershire player John Board, who died some years later on board the 'Kennilworth Castle' whilst en route from South Africa to England, also played this season, as did the Sussex professional Joseph Vine.

At the end of the season, in a match which was probably the last for London County, Charlie made his mark. Matched against Warwickshire, the team he did so well against in 1901, he made a splendid 102 not out.

He excited the crowd making his runs in fine style as his team was chasing victory. Unfortunately County did not achieve their aim, but Sinclair and Charlie put on 131 for the 6th wicket partnership. Charlie also took 2 wickets in each innings.

Amongst the participants in this game was J.W.H.T. Douglas, who played for London County in the last two seasons of its existence. Douglas was relatively unknown at the time, but his experiences with County helped him become one of the best all-rounders in the country.

Charlie McGahey ended his London County career on a high note. He had surely added sparkle to the surroundings. Colourful, charismatic characters like himself had blessed Crystal Palace with their presence, and it was a sad sight, indeed, to see the club disband.

Unfortunately, the attendances were never as good as initially expected. The many county players were obligated to their counties and, like Charlie, had to fit their attendances for County around these commitments. The Crystal Palace ground was in an isolated position, and the uncompetitive nature of the matches probably made it difficult for the regular supporters to identify with the club.

So much first-class cricket was available in London, and the sides tended to have their loyal supporters who followed their clubs through thick and thin. Regular players were always there to back up team performances, and the standard of play was probably more consistent.

W.G. Grace did not match up to expectations. Although highly regarded as an individual, his age was telling; way past fifty years of age, he was now losing some of his charisma. A committee meeting was held shortly after that match was played in August 1904 and it was decided to dissolve the club.

The man who epitomized 'all that is cricket' and sowed the seeds in every part of the empire had not made that much of a success of his final venture. He was nearing the last decade of life and did not want too much turmoil in the winter of his years. The threat of war and its final awareness was to prove too much for him, and in 1915 he was to breathe his last.

Charlie McGahey, though, must have been grateful to London County for giving him the opportunity to display his talents. Cricket was quick and eager, relying on plenty of action to hold spectators attention, and Charlie, of course, was always happy to obey these rules.

It was a recreation for him, away from the demands of county cricket; giving way to a carnival atmosphere he was able to relax to the full amongst some of the best cricketing characters of the time. Although selected for McLaren's team, he was never really up to standard, and perhaps selection for events such as these made up a little for his deficiency as a great national hero!

One wonders whether a similar side may emerge in the future. Certainly it would be interesting to witness such a sight! The idea has never been resurrected, and perhaps it is a dubious proposition. Kerry Packer, seventy years later, found, like the Crystal Palace authorities at the beginning of the century, that a circus such as this cannot exist if there is no 'partisan nucleus'. It seems 'cheery cricket' is not enough, nor is the presence of highly skilled participants. Cricket today is seemingly too competitive to put the future Charlie McGaheys' on a false pedestal even if it is only for a brief period of their cricketing careers.

5

Partnerships

' A man slow of speech, dour and heavy footed:' These were words used by Charles Bray to describe that huge man with a brilliant eye for fast bowling, Peter Perrin of the Essex Twins. A cautious, correct batsman, he scored over 29,000 runs for Essex in a long career stretching to 1928, when he played his last match for Essex at the age of fifty-two.

One always associated him with Charlie McGahey. They blended together like cheese and wine, the one complementing the other. Quieter, more introverted than Charlie, he was a deep thinker, and it was said of him that 'he doesn't always speak but when he does it's worth listening to'.

They both had a reputation for humour, but as Gerald French points out: 'Whereas in the case of McGahey it is sparkling and bubbly, Perrin tended to be a dry brand.' Perrin acted accordingly after the Essex defeat by Derbyshire in 1904; a match in which he scored 343 in the first innings and saw his team skittled out for 97 in the last innings. It prompted him to say: 'We wanted to show 'em, you see, in what we could do in each direction.' E.H.D. Sewell says of the twins:

> No other county ever had such a tall pair as the Essex Twins, Percy Perrin and Charlie Mc.Gahey. Both over 6ft, and both top-notcher batsmen, any two less like twins in character, temperament, looks and method you'd have a long march to find. They had practically nothing in common. Of them a blunt Sheffielder said: 'Well! All ah can say is as ah'd rather go fish in a blinkin' puddlehole nar watch they two-s a battin'.' That was of course, ultra-Yorkshire patriotism, after having watched these two defy Yorkshire's best bowling for hour after hour.

Perrin was five years younger than McGahey and began his

5. *McGahey showing he could also defend when necessary.*

career three years later, but they blossomed together, and as early as 1898 were beginning their series of famous partnerships.

On 4 July they played 'magnificently together', so said *The Leytonstone Express & Independent*, helping to impose a crushing defeat for Derbyshire by an innings and 172 runs. Essex made a marvellous 497 and, due to McGahey's 115 and Perrin's 104, were able to declare on this score for the loss of only 5 wickets. Derbyshire were absolutely humiliated, making only 166 and 159 in their two attempts at the crease.

This was a curtain-raiser to a match the following week which was to set the seal on the evidence of the twins working together and helping to achieve results.

Essex went to Old Trafford on July 14-15-16 and the magnificent performance of McGahey and Perrin brought off a spectacular win against the Lancashire side. *Wisden* says of this match:

> Essex' unprecedented achievement in their last innings was due to grand batting by McGahey and Perrin who put on 191 runs. Essex won by 4 wickets. Tyldesley and Sugg dominated the opening day, adding 169 runs for the 3rd wicket. Sugg made the large proportion of the runs, whilst Essex bowled well. The last 7 wickets fell for 48 runs.
>
> Essex began well in their first innings but by the time they faced their second innings they were set a tremendous task – 336 in order to win. On Friday evening they had made 34 without loss. Owen and Carpenter raised the total to 88, but Essex only achieved the great win by grand batting from the Essex Twins. Perrin made 61 whilst McGahey went on to score 145, adding 191 for the 3rd wicket.

This was the highest score by any Essex player this season. According to Charlie McGahey's obituary, it was described as, 'the best display of batting that he ever gave.' Charlie did make 115 against Derbyshire this year, as well as some credible 70s and a few 50s, so in all he had a very successful season.

Essex, though, did not have such a good year as the year before. All hopes of winning the championship after the very good year of 1897 easily faded. But both the twins passed the 1,000 run mark, and did much to help their side in achieving fifth position in the championship.

Another outstanding match attributed to the Essex Twins was a match at Leicester on 7-8-9 August 1899. The home team did not take full advantage of batting first and the whole side was out for 194, after Wood and Knight put on 74 for the first wicket.

Before close of play Essex were within 51 of their opponent's total for the loss of Carpenter. They ran up a score of 673 – the highest score ever made on the Aylestone Ground. It must be said that Fane was the real hero of the day, weighing in with a fine 207. Charlie hit hard for his 99, and his twin batted brilliantly for his 132 – making 16 fours in his attempt.

Leicester needed 479 – a mammoth task to achieve, especially batting last on a wearing wicket. Not surprisingly, half the side were dismissed for 73 runs. Knight saved face by making 111 and deserved the highest praise for his effort. Essex gained overwhelming victory by an innings and 223 runs in a most entertaining game!

Percy Perrin well remembered an instance of Charlie's quick thinking wit in this memorable match. Perrin was at the other end when Charlie was dismissed on 99. As Perrin recalled: 'He played at the next ball and said "come on" but failed in his stroke, and was bowled. As he passed by on the way to the pavilion he said to the bowler. "Lucky for you I wanted a drink." '

In a total of 35 innings, the most he had ever encountered, Charlie only managed to make 983 runs for Essex in 1899. His only century for his county was against Warwickshire, a fine knock of 130, although he did secure some good scores elsewhere. A Club and Ground match against Wanstead saw him make 105 and, for the North of the Thames Licensed Victuallers against the South in the annual September fixture at the Oval, he topped the scales with an excellent 133.

By this time the twins were quite inseparable. Charlie's loyalty to Perrin was such that he was even prepared to turn out for Perrin's own club Tottenham, against, of all sides Leyton, and on that very hot July day did not hesitate to rise to the occasion, making a very fine 108.

Although Essex were having a lean time in 1900 and their bowling was rather poor, causing them to slump even further in the championship to a meagre tenth position, Charlie McGahey was still batting well. Like Carpenter and Perrin, Charlie scored over 1,000 runs this season and shared a partnership with both batsmen.

He and Carpenter put on 235 for the third wicket at home to Sussex, but it was the 323 that Charlie made with Perrin which overshadowed the partnership with Carpenter, and, gained such publicity. What could be better than two amateurs at the crease! Especially, as the two popular gents had taken over from A.P. Lucas and H.G.P. Owen as the county's leading amateur rungetters.

Percy Perrin remembered that Kent, having fielded out 270 runs at the Oval without taking a Surrey wicket in the last stage of the drawn match, came to Leyton and lost the toss. 'They got two men out before lunch,' Perrin recalled, 'then McGahey and I batted the rest of the day.'

Charlie made 142, whilst Perrin dominated the proceedings with an excellent 205. At that time, it was a record for the 3rd wicket and prompted *Wisden* to write: 'This 323 partnership made in 4 hours was free from fault, but they sometimes carried caution to an extreme' . . . Harsh words perhaps for a partnership which maintained an average rate of scoring of 76 runs an hour!

Unfortunately there were many drawn games the following season. Two-thirds of Essex games were unfinished, which was due partly to the excellence of the Leyton wicket, which made the bowlers job rather difficult, and partly to the fact that the bowling was extremely weak.

Walter Mead, who took 122 wickets in 1900, was not so consistent, and Kortright, who took only 25 wickets at a cost of 40 runs apiece, was described by *Wisden* as 'a great disappointment'. George Bull, who had taken over 100 wickets in both 1897 and 1898, completely lost form and left the staff at the end of the 1900 season.

This did not distract from the fact that the twins and Harry Carpenter all managed to score prolifically. The 1,838 runs credited to Charlie were highly commendable, and he was well rewarded with a trip to Australia with A.C. McLaren's team in the Winter of 1901-02, as well as being selected as one of the five *Wisden* players of 1901.

His good partnership with Percy Perrin continued. They were engaged in an excellent stand for Tottenham, and this time they were up against club side Clapton. *Wisden* said of the game: 'Mr C.P. McGahey and Mr P.A. Perrin going in first scored 309 together without being separated for Tottenham versus Clapton on the latter's ground on 6 July 1901. The former made 168 not out and the latter 133 not out.'

Gloucestershire and Charlie went well together in 1901 and in both innings, at home and away, he managed to hit the high spots. At Bristol he made scores of 66 and 91, but it was at the Leyton match where history was made. Charlie made 114 and 145 respectively in the home match with Gloucester, and he became the first Essex amateur to make 100 in each innings of a first-class match.

He was, in fact, the first Essex player to ever accomplish this feat, an effort that much encouraged the professional Harry Carpenter. 'What an amateur could do so could a professional:' stated Carpenter, and he produced the goods in the second game of the same week by scoring a hundred in each innings versus Kent.

Harry 'Bob' Carpenter was a stylish opening bat and the son of Robert Carpenter, a prominent player in the 'heady days' when Cambridgeshire hailed as such a good team. He featured in quite a few stands for Essex, notably with both T.M. Russell and Charlie McGahey.

The 268 stand with Russell was a one-time record for the fourth wicket. Occurring against Derbyshire at Derby in 1900 it was not beaten until Jack O'Connor and Tom Pearce made 271 against Lancashire at Clacton in 1931. The one with Charlie took place in 1904, and it was a third wicket record at the Oval. Carpenter made 199 and Charlie 177. Curiously enough, like Charlie's partnership with Perrin versus Kent, this was another four-hour duel.

Charlie, along with Percy Perrin, continued to make good scores and their haul of 1,000 runs a season became a regular occurrence. The pair were the mainstay of the Essex team in the early years of the century and it must have been disheartening for them, prior to 1905, to see their club reach no higher than eighth position in the championship.

Talk to the average man at this time about Essex cricket and a certain picture came into his mind. Essex for him meant Leyton, a homely ground, dinginess, a brilliant wicket, and long drawn-out partnerships between Perrin and McGahey. If they did not share together in entertaining partnerships, they often displayed their talents separately; not wanting to outshine the other, but showing that they could both excel. This happened in 1904.

Charlie showed for the first time in 1904 that he was capable of staying the pace and remaining at the crease long enough to score a double century in one innings. He had made many centuries in his time, but it was always thought up until now that his big hitting was not conducive to an extremely long innings. Against Nottinghamshire at Leyton he proved his critics wrong, and matched against such skilful bowlers as T.G. Wass, the quick leg-break bowler, a rare commodity indeed, A.W. Hallam and J.R. Gunn, he came up trumps.

Although this score of 225 might have been impressive and entertaining to watch, it was not the talk of Essex at the end of the 1904 season. It was left to Percy Perrin to provide this; he was to supply us with an innings which made cricketing history, and left us in no doubt as to his polish as a batsman. The match versus Derbyshire at Chesterfield in July of that year not only provided Perrin with his highest score in first-class cricket, but also provided a feat without equal in that he was on the losing side.

There were only 12 runs on the board when Essex lost Carpenter, but a fine recovery was soon on the cards. Fane 63, McGahey 32 and Gillingham 43, rendered great support to Perrin, who from the start of his innings showed remarkable ease and speed.

There was a stand of over 100 for the third and fourth wickets and, although Derbyshire were not what one would call a good bowling side, they had in Bestwick and Warren, who the next season played for England against the Australians and took 5–53 in the Australian first innings at Headingley, two very good fast bowlers.

Three Essex wickets fell very cheaply before J.W.H.T. Douglas, in his infancy as an Essex all-rounder, helped to add 130 for the eighth wicket. He made 47 and E. Russell remained whilst 73 more were added to the total. Eventually, when the Essex innings closed on 597, it was realized that Perrin had scored his 343 not out in an incredible 345 minutes.

6. *McGahey in fine flow.*

He hit no fewer than 68 fours, and his score was, at that time, the fifth highest ever made in a first-class match. It is interesting to note that, by comparison with Hutton's 364 at the Oval versus the Australians in 1938, Perrin made only 21 fewer runs in seven and a half hours less time.

Such a high score should have insured the southern team against defeat, but the huge total amassed by Essex did not seem to worry the Derbyshire team in any way. They put on 191 and 128 respectively for the 1st and 2nd wickets and eventually reached 548, only 49 runs behind the Essex total. A brilliant 229 was rendered by C.A. Ollivierre, and L.G. Wright made 68. Seven other Derbyshire batsmen supported Ollivierre, and, with only a day left, it seemed that an almost certain draw was on the cards.

But Essex slumped terribly in their 2nd innings, Sewell 41, and Douglas 27 not out were the only two players to reach double figures, and Essex finished their dismal attempt on 97. In fact nine Essex batsmen made 25 between them. Such is the uncertainty of cricket that Perrin this time failed to score.

Derby were left with the enviable task of wanting only 147 to win. Ollivierre followed up his fine first innings score with 92 not out, and Derby hit the runs off for the loss of Wright, who was out for a single.

When asked several years later what he recalled of that magnificent innings Perrin drily answered: 'I strolled a few singles, trotted a few twos, and just leaned on my bat and watched the rest.' Although naturally upset in making such a big score and being on the losing side he was obviously not bitter.

If 1904 was the year of Percy Perrin then 1905 belonged to Charlie. As the *Essex Year Book* points out: 'Charlie McGahey returned to his best form with 1,783 runs, and during this season hit his highest innings in first-class cricket, 277 versus Derby at Leyton.'

Percy Perrin believed this was 'one of his greatest innings', 'a sheer joy to witness'. The twins, also, were to partake in a fine partnership of 233 against Middlesex at Lord's, and Perrin also went on to make 1,000 runs again this season.

Support was low, though, and once again it was a very poor

year for Essex. From fourteenth in the table in 1904 the side rose to twelfth this season, but in both years they won only three of their twenty games, losing ten and drawing seven.

On top of this, Walter Mead had a dispute with the club after he had requested an increase in his winter's pay. Essex missed his bowling immensely as he had not played for the club for a whole season. It can be said that the matter could have been handled better, as *Wisden* points out:

> On the face of it, an application for increasing pay during the winter on the part of such a valuable servant ought not to have led to a dispute. But unhappily the difficulty proved incapable of adjustment, the committee being only willing to take Mead back into the XI under conditions he could not see his way to accept.

But, on the other hand, there was talk of extinction. Essex was in grave financial difficulties, and had it not been for the generous donations of Mr C.E. Green, the then Essex President, at the end of each AGM, Essex would have faced extermination many years before.

By 1906 Mead had withdrawn his demands and the dispute was settled. The crowd at Leyton rallied round and gave increased support, whilst the team prospered and climbed to seventh in the table. This was the year that Essex beat Notts for the first time in their history. In this match Charlie made 89 and 14 respectively.

The highest innings of his career was also witnessed this year. Although not recorded as a first-class fixture, an Essex XI took on a Carmarthenshire side at Llanelly, on July 9-10, and a fine knock of 305 not out was recorded by Charlie McGahey.

Southchurch Park, in Southend, was added to the fixture list for the first time and became the first seaside venue for Essex cricket. Charlie came to love his visit to the seaside. Tents and deck chairs gave a cheery look to the lovely park, and its pretty boating-lake gave a pleasant diversion.

This was a time when the captaincy of Essex changed hands very rapidly. From 1894-1910 no fewer than five men held this post, the last being Charlie himself. All the other senior amateur players had had a stab at the captaincy and, when Charlie resigned in 1910, it was thought, by many, that Percy Perrin would be selected to fill the vacant role.

Perrin was then aged thirty-five, well liked, and the most senior amateur not to have captained the team. He had gained the reputation of being the best English batsman never to have played for his country. Even so, he was overlooked in favour of Johnny Douglas, who first played for Essex five years after Perrin, but whose father had come to the aid of the committee a few seasons before. Charles Kortright seconded Lucas in proposing that the job be offered to J. Douglas, and the Essex all-rounder led Essex until 1928.

Perrin expected to be captain, that is for certain. He declined to play for Essex in the first few weeks of Douglas' captaincy, and it took a great deal of gentle persuasion from others before common-sense prevailed. His own generous good nature eventually was put to good use, and in time he became a good friend and adviser to the younger man. Perrin would always use his humour to deflate a tense situation. On one occasion when Douglas was secretive about a team selection, Perrin enquired: 'Is Mrs Douglas playing today?'

Sir Home Gordon has his own reason for overlooking Perrin and made this clear in his book *Background of Cricket*, published in 1939. He believes Perrin would have led Essex but 'Old Douglas' held the mortgage on the Leyton Ground, and Douglas senior had intimated that he would foreclose if his son was not made captain.

Charles Bray, a friend and admirer of J.W.H.T. Douglas, is reluctant to believe the story, but admits father 'pulled strings'. The 'old man', as he was known, was very powerful and his gesture of donating £5,000 eased the immediate difficulties and saved the club in 1907-08 from certain extinction.

It appeared, also, according to Charles Sale in his book *Korty, the Legend*, that Charles Kortright was offered the captaincy at a committee meeting in February 1911. Kortright had played his last game for the club on 26 June 1907, claiming 489 wickets during his thirteen year career, and had captained the team briefly during the 1903 season.

Although it had been four years since he had played a first-class game he had showed he was still able to produce match-winning performances and had been on the committee since his captaincy days. Charles Sale says: 'After a month deliberating the matter Kortright decided it would be a retrograde step for him to skipper Essex again. He told the committee on 29 March that he could not accept their offer, and then seconded Lucas's proposal that the job be offered to Johnny Douglas.'

This incident coincided with the departure of C.E. Green, who resigned as Chairman of the club in the winter of 1912. Green felt that the game was changing and becoming more commercialized in favour of the professionals. He realized that the increase in fixtures to 24 each season would restrict the amateurs, as many of them would not be able to spare the time to play cricket regularly, resulting in an increase in the number of professionals, and an increase in match payments.

He felt he could no longer bail out Essex if this was to be the case. Green was surely saddened after a life-time's interest in the game. He stood down, and with him nearly the entire committee. John Douglas senior, accompanied by a loyal band of supporters, then took over the running of the club on a more commercially-minded basis.

In 1911, the county rose to sixth position. Perrin made 1,281 runs, but after this time 1,000 runs per season was not such a regular occurrence for him.

Charlie, meanwhile, was struggling. It was obvious to cricket lovers everywhere that his career was in decline; his age was telling, he seemed way past his best. But in 1912 a light was re-kindled when he and Perrin had a magnificent match against Derbyshire, a team they had so often come off well against.

Perrin made 245 and Charlie 150 in a classic third wicket partnership of 312 which took the 'old Essex supporter' back to the 'great days' at the turn of the century when the twins drew crowds from far and near. Perrin was aged thirty-six and Charlie forty-one, which made the feat even more remarkable.

Someone who remembered the game with affection is former Leyton FC committee member, Bill Cole. He knew Charlie as a cricketer, and also, in later years, at the Leyton FC ground at Brisbane Road, where Orient now play. Now a very fine and fit octogenarian, Bill Cole has vivid recollections of the game. Said Bill Cole: 'My happiest memory of Charlie McGahey was at the Whitsun Week-end match against Derbyshire in 1912 when he shared that 3rd wicket partnership with Percy Perrin, scoring 150 while Percy got 245.' Mr Cole continues: 'Essex amassed a total of 609–4 enabling them to win the only match they won that season. Charlie must have liked the Derbyshire bowling as he made his highest score against them of 277 in 1905. It was a matter of interest in that match that Derbyshire had two players called Beet and Root.'

One cannot make 29,172 runs, at an average of 36.19, without having a great many partnerships and making some good, hefty scores. Percy Perrin certainly achieved this. From 1899 when he and Fane made 235 for the second wicket away at Leicester, until he and Freeman made 200 at home for the fifth wicket against Oxford University in 1925, hardly a season went by when a good stand was not recorded.

In 1903, at Trent Bridge, he recorded 170 and 102 not out, at Lord's in 1905, 140 and 103, Trent Bridge, again in 1911, 112 and 100, and at Leyton versus Kent in 1919, 126 and 101. He made 65 centuries for his county and made 1,000 runs in a season seventeen times. But he never knew what it was like to wear an England shirt upon his back.

There seems to be two main reasons for this. Firstly, he was unfortunate enough to play at a time when there was a glut of good batsmen because, during the Golden Age, competition was strong. Secondly, according to C. Bray, 'he was slow, almost cumbersome in the field.' Bray continues:

> Even in his younger days he was not a fast-mover although his footwork when batting, particularly against fast bowlers, was excellent. An impression was created that he was a bad catcher as well, which is extremely wrong. Admittedly in his last few seasons Perrin missed a lot of chances being too slow to get to the ball, and often misjudging it when he did get his hands to it, but it is forgotten that he did play until fifty-two years of age. No-one could expect to have ability of limb and sureness of eye at that age. In his prime Perrin was an excellent catcher. He caught 173 during his career.

The man who gained the reputation of being the finest batsman never to have played for England would be the first to admit that fielding was not his strong point. Legend has it that when asked if he had really stopped one of Hobbs' boundaries down Vauxhall

Way he replied reasonably: 'Oh yes, mind you, they ran 8.'

This rather morose, reserved man took a great interest in cricket right up to his death. He could always spot a good youngster and was instrumental in discovering Ken Farnes and making Stan Nichols into such a capable fast-bowler.

The gods may not have shone brightly on Perrin during his playing career but honours did come his way in later life. In 1926 he became an England Selector and helped choose the 1926 England Team that regained 'the Ashes'. In 1931 he again took on the post. There was a clean-sweep of the Selection Committee, H.D.G. Leveson-Gower, F.T. Mann and J.C. White were thrown-out, and in their place came Sir Pelham Warner, P.A. Perrin and T.A. Higson. In 1939 he was appointed Chairman.

Legend has it that Charlie and Peter Perrin regularly caught the tram from Leyton Station, near the 'Three Blackbirds', to the county ground, and Charlie always ended up paying both fares. It is also said that Perrin rarely paid for a round of drinks, despite owning a string of East End pubs.

If Charlie was free and easy, not thinking of tomorrow, then Perrin was careful to plan, ensuring that his later days would be spent in reasonable comfort. Poverty was not to hamper him, and he did not have to consider working into 'old age', like Charlie, just to make 'ends meet'.

They were as different as chalk and cheese, and, like many working partnerships, tended to go their separate ways outside the game. They rarely frequented the same haunts, and yet there was a certain bond between them – an understanding that had been sealed many years before.

Both bachelors, they chose solitary lives, but when they came together on the cricket field another picture emerged. It is doubtful that Charlie would have been such a good player had it not been for Perrin.

Perrin survived his Essex twin by more than ten years; his death occurred on 20 November 1945 at Hickling, Norfolk, just as the game was emerging from the bitter years of war. He was 69.

6

The Cornstalks and the Pom

In 1901, Melbourne Cricket Club invited the MCC to send an official side to tour Australia. The MCC set about making arrangements, but on 13 May the committee announced at Lord's that it was impossible to recruit a representative England team as so many amateurs declined the venture. These included the three top batsmen in the 1901 averages; Fry, Ranjitsinhji and Palairet.

A.C. McLaren, the Lancashire captain, was then asked to send out a team. This was not an easy task. The Yorkshire committee failed to release Rhodes and Hirst, and so the bowling strength was bound to show some weakness.

Amongst the players eventually selected was a surprise candidate, S.F. Barnes. Unknown to the public at large Barnes had played most of his cricket in the Lancashire League, although he had played the odd game for Warwickshire and Lancashire. Jessop, Hayward, Tyldesley and Quaife were also in the team, as was an exceedingly tall, moustached gent named Charles Percy McGahey, who had just had the best season of his cricketing career to date.

Although described by Sewell as 'an ungainly bat', on his best day, in May 1901 for example, Charlie averaged something like 150. A sure run-getter, very hard to get out and a straight driver, it was no real surprise that he should be picked after the top three batsmen declined the tour. His fielding ability had also been witnessed, notably in the Lancashire versus Essex match at Leyton in mid-August when he threw the ball in from long-on with such force that a stump was broken.

He had excelled in the summer of 1901, but at a price. Tuberculosis had set in and the trip to Australia was a recuperative measure as well as a serious affair. It meant refusing the opportunity to play soccer for his old club Clapton, but he

7. England team aboard the SS Omrah, 1901–02.
Back Row: J. Gunn, C. Blythe, S. F. Barnes, A. A. Lilley, T. W. Hayward, L. C. Braund.
Middle Row: H. G. Garnett, C. P. McGahey, A. C. Maclaren (Captain)., C. Robson, A. O. Jones. Front: W. G. Quaile, J. T. Tyldesley.

could not turn down the chance to go to 'sunnier climes'.

The team left Tilbury on board the SS Omrah on 27 September 1901 only to be welcomed six weeks later in Adelaide by rain. Unfortunately, Charlie was not to experience a heatwave as in 1897. Dull days were to accompany himself and the team throughout the tour.

It took a while for the tourists to adjust after their journey and they were defeated in their first match on Australian soil, but the second match saw the team secure a win. Charlie played in this match making 57 runs in a very low scoring game against the Victorian State side. The scores were England 166 and 174, Victoria 133 and 89; the State side losing to England by 118 runs. Barnes, the surprise selection, was too much for Victoria, taking 5–61 and 7–38.

Charlie did not play again until the seventh match of the tour when England took on the might of Newcastle, an up-country team in the mining town of the same name. The game took place between 7-9 December and, in the first innings for the tourists, Charlie made 52 of the 315 runs mustered. In the second innings Jessop scored 85 of their 216. Newcastle could only reply with 241 and 73–0, so the match petered out into an uneventful draw.

In spite of Charlie's 52 in the Newcastle match he was not selected for the 1st Test Match. This began on 13 December and was played in Sydney. From the outset Anglo-Australian cricket matches created an element of nationalistic rivalry. After all, cricket had been very much part of the process of empire-building, and Australia would fight desperately against her subservient background, ensuring that a tough, but chivalrous contest would always be on the cards.

In this particular Test match England got away to a magnificent start. McLaren scored 116 and batted brilliantly, something that he was so often to do abroad, whilst Lilley made an excellent 84. Tom Hayward, scored 69, and Len Braund 58. With a total of 464 on the board, the tourists were unbeatable.

Australia had a massive task in front of them. After making 168 in the first innings, Barnes taking 5–65, it was an uphill struggle. Braund tore the second innings apart, taking 5–61, and the tourists scored a decisive victory winning by an innings and 124 runs.

The Australians played their game hard, and Charlie was quick to point out years later to Tom Cable that what A.E. Stoddart referred to as 'loud voiced satire and banter' was greatly in evidence. All the more so when Australia was on the losing side.

Back home, interest was rife. A scoreboard was set up outside the *Daily Mail* and *Herald* offices in Fleet Street, and euphoria set in as the game was pointing more and more in England's favour. This certainly whetted the appetite of the average Englishman who was eager to believe a 'walk-over' was in store.

After the celebrations the tourists moved on to Goulbourn for their final match before Xmas. The match played on 20 and 21 December gave Charlie a chance to show his worth. Charlie made 55 out of 192 in the tourist's first innings, whilst Goulbourn replied with 190, Jones taking 10–49. England went on to defeat the small-town side by 6 wickets.

The 11th match of the tour was the 2nd Test Match. This time Melbourne was the setting and, once again, Charlie was a spectator. The match was particularly low scoring in the first innings. Australia made 112 runs, Barnes taking 6–42; whilst England made only 61 in their attempt. The 'Cornstalks' replied with 353, leaving England a massive task. The tourists could only manage 175 in their second innings, which resulted in an humiliating defeat by 229 runs.

Charlie did not participate in the following two matches, nor was he picked for the 3rd Test Match at Adelaide. He must have felt dejected and very disappointed. His team-mates had just lost a Test match, and they needed to win this game in order to go one up in the series. Charlie must have thought that a hard-hitter such as himself was worth trying, as more successful players had failed.

The match which started on 17 January saw England make 388 in the first innings. Braund scored a magnificent 103, Tom Hayward an excellent 90, Quaife 68 and McLaren 67. With a grand total such as this it must have seemed impossible to have been beaten. The Australians replied with 321. Clem Hill just missed his century with a remarkable 98, and was ably backed by the classic Victor Trumper, who made a fine 65.

The tourists in their second innings made 247, with Hugh Trumble taking 6–74. It seemed a mighty task for the home team who needed 315 when starting the last innings of the match.

Unfortunately for England both Barnes and Blythe were hurt during the course of the match. When Australia went in to bat Barnes was in bed nursing an injured knee, and Blythe, the artistic slow left-arm bowler, was handicapped by a broken finger.

Clem Hill was 'in form' and took full advantage of the situation amassing 97 with comparative ease. Joe Darling played a captain's innings of 69, and Trumble, not to be left out, made 62. The Australians knocked off the 315 with the loss of only 6 wickets, and the tourists could only hang their heads in shame.

Charlie was now given his chance. He was selected for the game following the Test Match on 25 January against a Victorian State side. The England side amassed 377 for the loss of 6 wickets before declaring on a high note. Quaife was there with 91, and the reliable Hayward made 57, but Charlie weighed in with a fine 79, reminding the selectors that he was a force to be reckoned with.

The Country team made only 111 in its first innings and, being forced to follow on, could only manage 267 at the second attempt. The tourists were then left to make 2 runs. This win must have gone some way to restoring confidence. It must also have helped Charlie, as he knew he was capable of scoring runs.

Charlie was lucky again when he was selected on 7 February for the match against Bathurst. This was the last game before the 4th Test match and, for the tourists, an opportunity to get in some batting practice. England made 505, with Charlie finishing on 71. The game petered out to a dull draw, but it must have put the lads in a good mood for the all-important fourth Test.

So the time had come for Charlie McGahey to make the greatest debut of his cricketing career. On 14 February he was chosen to play in the 4th Test Match at the great Sydney Cricket Ground. Darling had relinquished the captaincy of the Cornstalks for business reasons, and Hugh Trumble took over. Barnes had a try-out in the nets before the start of the game but declared himself unfit for the match. On the brighter side, Archie McLaren won the toss for the fourth consecutive time.

Along-side such great names as Archie McLaren, Gilbert Jessop, and J. Tyldesley, Charlie pulled on an England sweater, placed his England cap upon his head and, when his turn came, went out on to the Sydney Cricket Ground to face up to the might of the Australian bowlers. The England side mustered 317 in its first innings. McLaren made 92 of these runs, but Charlie could only manage a meagre 18, and was clean bowled by Hugh Trumble.

Jessop, bowling at his fastest, caused an early upset. Three batsmen were brilliantly caught at slip and, when Jessop came off at 53–4, he had bowled 9 overs for 25 runs, and taken all four wickets. England had more than re-established the position their early batting had won for them. Then Noble, Duff and Armstrong, batting in solid style, began a recovery. Jessop was brought back but could not recapture his early pace.

With the onset of rain play finished early, with Australia on 148-5. Noble had batted 2 hours 24 minutes before reaching 50, and England soon dismissed the two not out batsmen on the third morning.

At lunch Australia were 201–7, but then the tail-enders hit out successfully. Howell made 35 in 14 minutes with Australia having got within 18 runs of England's total.

Psychologically, from this time onwards, Australia had the upper hand, perhaps explaining England's otherwise unaccountable collapse on a good wicket. The side had been subjected to a magnificent piece of out-cricket. Noble and Saunders had bowled unchanged, and they were backed-up by keen fielding and brilliant wicket-keeping.

Australia had a complete stranglehold on the game by stumps on the third day when England had scored 77–7. England went on to finish on a hopeless 99, 13 of these runs were scored by the luckless McGahey.

A demoralized England side dropped many catches and fielded ruggedly, and Australia lost only 3 wickets in knocking off the 118 needed to defeat the tourists. England had played badly and allowed the Australians to win the series and, whatever happened in the 5th Test match, the damage was done, and England would return home in despair.

On 28 February, the tourists, tired and distraught, faced the might of the Antipodean Hemisphere for the last time. The Australian side did not have Darling and, to add salt to the wounds, decided to leave out the highly successful Saunders, whilst England decided to field an unchanged side.

Charlie must have been pleased to have been given a second

chance. He had failed on his debut, but so had many players greater than himself, and his colleagues had not exactly excelled themselves. He no doubt believed he could distinguish himself amidst the paramount splendours of Melbourne's fine ground, and must have hoped for better things prior to his return to English soil.

Australia won the toss for the first time in this series and on a moist wicket, heavily soiled with rain, elected to bat first. The wicket, initially, assisted the bowlers and Australia was dismissed in under 3 hours with only 144 on the board.

England's reply started well with Jessop opening the batting with McLaren. The 50 came up easily, although a collapse was soon to follow. By the close of play on the first day the tourists were 133–5.

The effects of the roller allowed the wicket to play faster and better as the following day progressed. Braund and Lilley took their unbroken stand to 68, but poor Charlie was no match for Trumble, once again, and was clean-bowled without a run to his name. England totalled 189 at the close of its innings, whilst Australia, in reply, was 128–2 at tea, and ploughed on to leave England a target of 211 to win.

Heavy showers further affected the wicket, necessitating more interruptions for rain during the third day. McLaren and Hayward made a steady start, and when play was curtailed at the end of the day England on 87–3, needed 124 to win.

The outfield was dead, and the ball was apt to kick off a length. Wickets tumbled. The last man joined Tyldesley and 50 were still wanted. When Tyldesley fell, the pair had put on 17, giving the Cornstalks a win by 32 runs. Noble and Trumble bowled unchanged exploiting the wicket to the full. England's batting was again in tatters, and like Stoddart's team of 1897-98, had been devastated.

Charlie was out to a good ball from Noble when making 7, hitting out, the ball fell into the very capable hands of Clem Hill. His two Tests had been a disaster. But no-one could take his two England caps away; no-one could deny him a place in the history books as a national player. He could attach the prefix England to his status now, a feat he was much proud of in the years ahead.

Wisden states: 'He took part in 2 Test Matches without much success, and generally on the tour he failed to produce anything like his full ability.'

An article on him in the *Essex Year Book* reiterates this, saying: 'He failed very badly, making only 210 runs with an average of 21 in the first-class matches, while his 4 Test innings' produced only 38 runs.'

Of course, many of the matches he played in were not first-class, perhaps showing that he was being used at times when the more accomplished players were being rested. But many other players had failed on the tour as well. The Australians were not a great team in the eyes of the critics, who were of the opinion that A.E. Stoddart's team of 1897-98 would have brought home the Ashes with comparative ease.

The England side won bouquets for its fielding; Jessop, Braund and McLaren were particularly outstanding. Only McLaren and Hayward, of the batsmen, came off, whilst Jessop, Jones and Gunn were complete failures. The bowling relied too heavily on Sydney Barnes, whose injury impeded the tourists to a great degree. If the series was famous for anything, it was for discovering this great bowler who the cricketing public was to hear so much about in the years ahead.

On the plus side, the experience was superb. In fact cricket interrupted the flow of social amenities. The team was somersaulted into a huge whirl of events as it moved from town to town. Receptions and banquets abounded, with the flow of drink much in evidence. As Jessop pointed out: 'Australia had much to teach England in cricket organization.'

Before setting sail at Fremantle, Western Australia, for the passage home, some light recreation was planned, and Charlie, for once, was one of the star attractions.

A soccer match was arranged with some local enthusiasts and McGahey, Lilley, Quaife and Gunn were the only players chosen who had experience of the league game. The rest of the England team had barely kicked a ball. Still the game provoked much excitement, and was billed as the first soccer 'International' between England and Australia.

Organized football in Australia dates from the early 1880s; the Anglo-Australian Association was formed as long ago as 1884. For more than fifty years soccer was a very poor relation to the Rugby

League game, so popular in New South Wales and Queensland, and to the Australian Rules Game, which is the number one sport in Southern Australia. The word 'soccer' is included in the title of the senior governing body, The Australian Soccer Football Association, to differentiate between Association Football and the local Australian Rules Game.

The result of the match in question was a win for England by 3 goals to 1, and the England side was 'in great spirits' for the journey home. The 'Aussie' weather had been reminiscent of home and, by March, the hope was for a pleasant Spring back home, and the start of another great cricket season.

On the soccer side, it was hoped the match would be repeated again some time. Gilbert Jessop was invited by the Australian Soccer Football Association to send out a team organized by the British Football Association in 1903. It was proposed that the English team would have a tour of Western Australia and show the young clubs how the game should be played. Unfortunately, however, nothing came of this proposal.

7

Back Home

As Charlie made his way back to London's East End, and to some of the people who had never set foot outside the dark and desolate paths of Leyton and Forest Gate, he reminisced, as he was to tell Tom Cable many years later, over the tales he could tell. There were huge banquets at grand and regal hotels, and the sights of the kangaroo, the wallaby and the aborigine, all so different from home. Even the outback and the cosmopolitan Australian were delights to ponder over as the SS Omrah made her sure, but steady voyage home.

He engaged in deck-games and lazed in the sun, happy in the company of some of the most endearing characters in cricketing history. Tom Hayward, the likeable Surrey professional, who did so much to inspire the great Jack Hobbs, impressed him immensely, as did the strong and capable Tyldesley, who could always be relied upon. Charlie was thrilled by the majesty of the 'croucher' himself, Gilbert Jessop, of whom a Philadelphian newspaper once called 'the human catapult who wrecks the roofs of distant towns when set on his assault'. Like Charlie, he played for London County (1900–1903).

Then, there was the captain himself. Archie McLaren was a stern, Victorian gent, whom the Australians regarded as the best batsman England had sent to their shores. He would dominate any attack in his grand determined manner, but was always a valued friend and adviser to the younger men in his team. Charlie found him a charming companion, and McLaren knew the benefits of the tour for Charlie, particularly as a recuperation from the effects of consumption.

As R.H. Spooner points out in McLaren's obituary in the *Times*, 25 November 1944: 'He never thought of himself, and there was no-one stricter in seeing that cricket was always played as it should be. He was a universal favourite, and never more so than in Australia.'

Many of the Australians were already legends, and Charlie was always ready to tell in later years how 'he felt overriding pride in making such good friendships.'

Hugh Trumble, born in 1867, was one of the oldest Australians in the side. He was a towering man who, like Charlie, used his height to full advantage when bowling his slow medium off spinners. With his superb control he could devastate pitches that were not suitable to his style of bowling.

Known as the 'ambling camel', his pedigree to date was outstanding, with truly remarkable figures of 12 wickets for 89 runs at the Oval in 1896. He took 148 wickets on that tour, at an average of 15.81, whilst in 1899 he was top of the bowling averages once again.

He was also a great slip fielder and a capable batsman; at least capable of holding up one end when necessary. McLaren, hardly known to praise, considered him to be, 'the most consistently excellent bowler ever encountered.'

Another great competitor, Clem Hill, was probably the finest left-hand batsman of his day. A fierce hitter, who crouched slightly at the wicket, he delighted in batting for batting sake and not just to score runs. With the grace of a dancer his defence was his attack, and he was capable of driving deliveries with extreme power through the on-side fielders.

Charlie would remember, in days-to-come, the sight of Hill and Victor Trumper throwing the ball from one side of the playing area to the other. This would happen at the fall of a wicket, a ritual performed with great ease. They were both great showmen, and they loved to undertake pursuits which would give added pleasure to the spectators.

Clem was thick-set with a solemn face and merry eyes. A first-rate sportsman he had an alert mind, and was nicknamed 'the kruger' after his supposed likeness to a Boer warrior. He had first played for Australia in 1896, and was 'the youngster' of the team on that occasion. Ill-health had deprived him of two games, but otherwise he played in every Test match to date. Hill liked to bat at number three and had already scored 1,304 runs at an average of 44.97 against England.

One cannot mention the Australians without thinking of their heavily-moustached, blue-eyed captain; his rolling gait, reminiscent of a countryman, eluded his air of confidence. His dry sense of humour was much in keeping with Charlie's, and he was a great guide to any young player. Darling was made a player of the year by *Wisden* in 1900, and had made three centuries in the 1897–98 series with England, at an aggregate of 537 runs. On the 1899 tour of England he made a record 1,941 runs, at an average of 61.29.

Victor Trumper was, by far, the most dazzling character on the tour. He was a most polished batsman who could score runs at a rate of over 60 an hour, on all kinds of pitches, and in all types of conditions, as well as against any attack of bowling. A brilliant hitter and attacker of the ball, he never played himself in, but could drive, cut or pull the bowlers off their length from the first ball he received. An added attraction was that, despite his achievements at the wicket and on the field, Trumper remained unspoilt, modest, generous and compassionate. An Edwardian professional cricketer wrote of him, 'that spirit, so self-forgetful, so manly and so true.'

On a cold April day in Edward VII's coronation year, the SS Omrah finally docked at Tilbury. It was time for 'the pommies' to say their goodbyes, go their separate ways, and return to their respective counties to prepare for another English season.

Charlie returned to Leyton with his two England caps to display, along with the many stories which made this tour so memorable. Also, about this time, he would have heard that his splendid season in 1901 was to be rewarded with the highest accolade possible in cricket, a *Wisden* player of the year. He was riding high, and must have wondered if he could start the 1902 season where he had left off in 1901.

The Australian touring team, meanwhile, began the preparation for their forthcoming tour. The previous Australian team to visit our shores, captained again by Darling, had handsomely beaten the flower of English cricket by winning the only completed match of the rubber, and had impressed us enormously.

Joe Darling was not sure of making the 1902 trip due to business commitments. He had recently moved from South

Australia to Tasmania to take up sheep-farming and, in his absence, the captaincy would have gone to the tall and strong bowler, deadly Hughie Trumble. Trumble had led Australia in the previous two Test matches in his own country, and had previously visited England on four occasions.

Many, in Australia, thought the team was not as strong as it may have been. Joe Darling, though, was confident in his team, and they with themselves and their astute captain. Major Benjamin J. Hardell, secretary of Melbourne Cricket Club, accompanied the team as manager, and the tour had been arranged by the Melbourne Cricket Club in conjunction with trustees of the Sydney Cricket Club – responsible for inviting Stoddart's 1894 and 1897 sides and McLaren's recent venture to Australia.

On Thursday 15 May, the Australians came to Leyton. They had been beaten by Essex in 1899, in what was a surprise victory. But now, although there was strength in the Essex batting line-up, the bowling was not up to the 1899 standard. Korty, 'Sailor' Young, and Walter Mead were all past their best, and Claude Buckenham had not been chosen.

To add to this, the weather at the end of April and in early May was wintry even by English standards. There was sleet and hail, and temperatures were little above 32 degrees that Spring. When it changed, it rained.

Two water-logged fixtures preceded this game for Essex; one versus Surrey at the Oval, and the other at Leyton, as host to Yorkshire. With one completed innings in each match the Essex batsmen did not have an opportunity to prove anything of note; Perrin and McGahey had made 42 and 48, both not out in the Surrey match, and Yorkshire dismissed the home side for 89 at Leyton.

Play was not possible until after 3pm, and the pitch was soft and difficult. Fane and Bob Carpenter were quickly dismissed with only 25 runs on the board, but once Perrin and McGahey were at the wicket the game changed. They made light work of a bad wicket and added 83 excellent runs.

Charlie was on his home ground now and must have been much more at ease, coupled with the fact that he was partnering his famous twin once gain. He managed to make a good 36, before being caught off Trumper when the score was on 108.

After a late start on Friday, the second day, Essex were finally removed for 178. In Australia's first innings Trumper made only 9, bowled by Young, and, by the time the skies opened again, only 70 minutes play had been possible. It was a really miserable day for players and spectators alike with only the prospect of a good innings by Hill to brighten events.

The third day brought a good start, and the previous day's expectations were fulfilled from an Australian point of view, with Hill making a good score. Charlie had a part to play in the proceedings but, for most of the Essex team, the day was more of a disappointment.

Charlie kidded Reg Duff into thinking he was bowling leg-breaks, and this enabled Russell to stump Duff when he had made 47. The Australians were then 200–4, with Hill on 100. Charlie was soon to take three successive catches; firstly Hill went on 104 (209–6), then Jones, and finally Howell (210–8). What an excellent fielder Charlie had now become! He was now quite accomplished in all three departments of the game.

When the match was abandoned, due to more rain, Charlie was not out 0 and Perrin not out 1. It was unlucky for the tourists because Essex may not have lasted long on that pitch, but, at least, Charlie had nothing to be ashamed of, and showed his worth as a good county player.

The Australians had already clinched the rubber when they visited Essex for the second time on the tour. The Cornstalks were tired, and could have done with a rest, but they had to spend their rest day travelling down from Manchester to Leyton by train.

Essex were not experiencing a great season, but were in good spirits after beating Derbyshire by 120 runs. This was only their second win of the season and, in the wake of this, the local people were looking forward to a good contest with the touring side after rain ruled the day in the previous game.

The Australians were weary and it showed in their play, allowing the Essex side to put on a good score. Lucas and Fane made a great start, putting on 26 and 81 respectively, before the twins prepared for business.

Perrin made 45, while Charlie rewarded the crowd with a fine 72 before being clean-bowled by Trumble. It was good to see

Charlie coming off against the Australians who had given him such a torrid time on the recent Antipodean tour. The crowd had probably come to see the local lad and were no doubt proud of him. Kortright made a good 66, and the remainder made a steady score culminating in 345 at the close of the innings.

If the spectators had come to witness Charlie McGahey as the 'wonder boy' of Essex cricket, they would also have come to witness Victor Trumper, the mainstay of Australia. The season in England had been long and triumphant for him so far, and the contest with Essex was to be no exception. Of 232 made in Australia's first innings Trumper mustered 109 and supporters of the game in Essex were privileged to see such a spectacle.

In the Essex second innings runs were slow in coming. Although the Leyton pitch was good, it took the team most of the final day to accumulate 184 runs before declaring for the loss of 3 wickets; Charlie making 59 before being caught by Noble off Jones.

Trumper really went for the runs once it was time for Australia to bat again. He made 119 before falling lbw to Bill Reeves. His two centuries in a match was a feat performed for the first time by a player in an Australian touring side.

Apart from these two centuries he made eleven others on the tour, one of these in a Test match at Old Trafford before lunch. In a year that saw bowlers everywhere taking the honours, Trumper was in a class of his own, scoring 2,570 runs, his highest total being 128.

The tourists got within 45 runs of the required target and had 4 wickets in hand at the end of the day. They were helped by Hill who made an able 59 before falling to Young. He was caught by the magnificent McGahey enjoying a great game.

By the time September arrived the tour was hailed as a great success. If the Australian XI did not quite pull it off on their two visits to Leyton they were certainly victors of their tussles with England.

Illness had demoralized the side slightly. Influenza had affected five members of the team in the first part of the tour, and the wet and cold conditions could not have helped matters. To add to this, Hughie Trumble injured the thumb of his bowling hand at practice before the start of the first match of the tour.

No doubt, Victor Trumper had a great part to play in their success. When he seemed dejected, which was only very occasionally, it seemed to affect the entire team. Conditions suited the Australians and all important lady-luck was always on her side. The Cornstalks received hearty congratulations and no doubt England and her cricketers were sad to see them depart for home.

Charlie was probably no exception. Disappointed, perhaps, not to have been chosen for the International matches he realistically would have come to terms with the state of affairs knowing that he was not quite up to Test standard. Though, having said that, he certainly did not upset any of his followers in either of the games in which he participated against the tourists. He enjoyed the battles with the 'old enemy', and he nearly always had something to contribute in these meetings. *The Essex Year Book* has this to say about his performances against the Australians:

> Inspite of his failure in Australia, McGahey had quite a good record against them, over 400 runs in 11 innings, including 72 and 59 in 1902. He was prominent in the 2 wins in 1899 and 1905. In the first mentioned, Essex lost their 3 second innings wickets for 8, then McGahey and A.J. Turner put on 93, and Essex eventually won by 126 runs. While in the 1905 game, his 39 was the highest Essex score and helped in a 19 run win; Essex being the only county to defeat the Australians on that tour.

Charlie had much to thank Australia and its touring teams. His trip out there broadened his horizons and gave him two International caps, whilst his experiences of the Cornstalks enriched his life.

In his final years he would often, when his landlady was away, spend Sundays at the Conservative Club in Leyton, which happened to be opposite the county ground. Mrs Swanton, whose father was then steward of the club, remembers Charlie and the tales he would tell about his tours. Even though she was only around ten years of age at the time she realized how important the trips of 1897 and 1902 were to him. He may have known poverty in the autumn of his days but he had memories to call on, and it was all apparent that he felt a better person for knowing Australia and its people.

8

Captaincy and Beyond

In 1907, the year that Charlie first captained Essex, the weather was far from good, but the county managed to retain its seventh position in the championship. Walter Mead topped the bowling averages with 120 wickets at a cost of only 16 runs apiece, and Douglas continued to improve, taking 72 wickets and batting more consistently. The Essex Twins took the batting honours, both scoring over 1,000 runs, with Perrin top of the county's averages with 35.90 and Charlie second with 34.12.

Amongst Charlie's scores were 59 and 74 against Nottinghamshire at Trent Bridge, 108 versus Kent at Tunbridge Wells, and a good 96 against Gloucestershire at Leyton. He was described in *Wisden* as 'one of the best batsmen in 1907,' confirming that the duties and responsibilities of captaincy in no way affected his game.

Edward Sewell said in his book *Cricket and How to play it:* 'Captains are not only born they are made.' He continues: 'They can be made by a close and constant study of the game. It used to be said that a captain's chief duty is to win the toss, but I think a much more important one combines seeing that his team is cheerful and happy, while at the same time making it play the game seriously.'

Charlie was certainly held in high regard by Sewell. Sewell played under five captains during his years as a player with Essex, and says: 'Of these C.J. Kortright and C.P. McGahey were easily the best. Charlie captained Essex very well indeed, and was very nice to me from start to finish, doing his utmost to make what could easily have been a fairly rough time as pleasant as possible.'

When Charlie succeeded Fane as captain assumptions were made by the committee that a change in captaincy might improve matters. Public support had waned during Fane's brief time as captain, and the committee warned 'all and sundry' that unless support improved matters would 'have to be wound up'. The team played better and the financial pressures eased temporarily, and in Fane's last year as captain the team managed to jump from twelfth to seventh position in the table.

By the 1907-08 winter, though, the financial crisis, which had affected the club for years, came to a head. It looked as if the club would have to be wound up and losses cut, until J. Douglas, father of J.W.H.T., came to the club's assistance by taking up one of the mortgages on the ground. This was for £5,000, and it allowed the immediate difficulties to be overcome.

The club won only five of its twenty-two matches in 1908, whilst 1909 was even worse. The team won only two of the eighteen matches played, both against Derbyshire, and they dropped even further, to fourteenth in the table. In fact, only Derbyshire and Gloucestershire were below them.

By 1910 matters were improving. The side had climbed back to eleventh place, and the bowling strength at last had some backbone. Essex won five matches out of seventeen and beat the then champions, Kent, at Leyton.

Essex beat Yorkshire convincingly in two days. Yorkshire made 152 and 130 and Essex 277 and 6–0. Mead took 7–75, whilst Buckenham, who was showing himself to be one of the best fast-bowlers in the country, weighed in with 5–68 in the first innings. Essex won by 10 wickets – some achievement!

Tremlin staged a come-back. His 62 wickets cost 20 runs each. Mead returned to form, while Percy Perrin had a bout of lumbago which upset his temper as well as his batting.

It seemed like the end of an era; Edward VII died, and the 'Twilight Age' emerged. Charlie McGahey, at nearly forty years of age, was facing the autumn of his years in cricketing terms, and at the end of the 1910 season, resigned the captaincy.

Charlie had been a 'trier', even if, at times, he had found the responsibilities of captaincy exhausting. He injured his hand at the beginning of the 1909 season, which meant he played for much of the year under a great handicap, but despite this he made 719 runs. 1910 saw him make even more runs. He scored 880, making 60 and 51, both not outs, in the Derby match, so he did not exactly disgrace himself.

However, Johnny Douglas, the new Essex captain, did have a good effect on the team. It won eight out of eighteen games and finished sixth in the championship in 1911. Unfortunately, his luck did not hold out. The following two seasons were very depressing, and matters did not improve until 1914 when the side climbed to 8th position.

'Jack' Russell scored 1,429 runs in 1914, and Johnny Douglas had improved his position. For the first time he had performed the double. He made 1,288 runs and took 138 wickets.

This was the year that Charlie severed his official links with Essex CCC. His good work over the years did not go unnoticed and the county decided upon a Testimonial for their loyal servant. In March 1914, a circular was issued by the Essex CCC stating that:

> After 21 years, Mr. Charles McGahey has terminated his official connection with the Essex County Cricket Club, and it has been felt that the time has arrived when his long and valuable services should be recognized. With this object in view, a small committee of the county club has been formed to promote a Testimonial Fund, the proceeds of which the committee will invest or utilize for Mr McGahey's benefit.

Also, war was declared in 1914. *Wisden* records: 'At the beginning of August 1914 county cricket was going splendidly, but the war, of course, upset everything.' Charlie escaped its rigours, but it brought his active life to a sudden halt.

The break allowed him to re-charge his batteries for the final surge before retirement, but he must have felt life was quite dull, especially as he no longer had his office duties to perform. Life in the pub went on as usual, and there were always faces appearing who needed 'cheering up', but dismal clouds hung low on the horizon, and it must have been a welcome relief when armistice sounded and life could continue as normal.

There was serious concern amongst the game's administrators whether the enthusiasm felt for the game prior to 1914 would be upheld. The standards and beliefs, much a part of the game in the earlier days, were no more, and the cosy world from which the amateur could escape the harsher realities of life had disintegrated.

Much thought went into the various changes that could be made to the game, and many suggestions were made during discussions at Lord's. The idea that boundaries should be shortened was one proposal, whilst another was that batting sides should be penalized for maiden overs. Ludicrous ideas like banishing left-handers and limiting professionals to four in each county side were considered, and it seemed that cricket's establishment body was unsure of the destiny of our summer sport.

In February 1919 it was decided that the two day game should replace the three day fixture and, not surprisingly, it turned out to be a disaster. It was difficult to achieve a result on good pitches without declarations, and quite impossible for teams without good batting line-ups.

1919 was an extremely fine summer and this made a complete mockery of the championship. Match after match was drawn. Twelve out of Essex' eighteen matches were unfinished and only two were won. The county finished fourteenth out of fifteen. Worcester did not compete this season and, for Essex, it was a year best forgotten.

Charlie McGahey was forty-eight years of age. Not only did he have to adjust to playing again after a five year break, but he also had the shorter game to contend with. This was good from the point of view that he did not have to soldier on for three days in succession, but difficult as more work had to be done in less time.

It is unlikely that Charlie would have played again if the game had not re-started so soon. As it was he had many difficulties to overcome. The environment had changed technically and psychologically, and the batsmen of the Golden Age were called upon to solve fewer problems of attack.

Fundamental brainwork was the order of the day in 1919 and would become even more important in the years ahead. Defensive and offensive field placings were not so flexible in the early days, and seldom did off-spin bowlers attack from around the wicket. To add to this, there was no new ball until the end of the longest innings.

Also, the game was devoid of many familiar faces. Hutchings of Kent, Percy Jeeves of Warwickshire and Major Booth of Yorkshire did not return from war. 1917 saw the demise of the great spin-bowler, Colin Blythe, whilst Reggie Schwarz and Gordon White were added to the list.

The preceding five years had also claimed many grand knights of cricket due to natural causes. That 'grand old man' of cricket, W.G. Grace, was no more, and Victor Trumper had perished from the effects of Bright's Disease, whilst A.E. Stoddart's suicide stunned all.

The Wisden Almanack of 1916 was most rare as it had eighty-two pages of obituaries. A host of excellent amateurs had perished, and Charlie would have been one of the grand veterans left in first-class cricket. It was now up to mature masters such as himself to lead the way and nurture the younger members entering the game. His kind, caring and thoughtful disposition would have been welcomed by many, and no doubt his attributes helped to instil confidence in others.

Charlie participated in only 10 innings and made 166 runs that season, taking no wickets. The Essex batsman probably imagined that his days of prominence were over, and that he was never again to steal the limelight. This, happily, was not to be the case. Although his days were numbered, as he definitely could not play for ever, he was to be much in focus during the 1920 season.

Raymond Robertson-Glasgow was definitely to remember Charlie in 1920. He was someone who would not forget him until his dying day. Robertson-Glasgow was a good, young fast-bowler in those days, and played in the Oxford University side that beat mighty Middlesex by 139 runs.

It was in the wake of this victory that Essex visited Oxford to play in a doubly notable fixture. Firstly, Douglas Jardine, playing for Oxford in his early days in first-class cricket, returned remarkable figures during an excellent spell of bowling. In 7 overs and 3 balls he took 6 for 6, including the great Percy Perrin for 0.

Secondly, Robertson-Glasgow was to acquire a nickname which was to stick for the rest of his life. That unique figure among the brotherhood of cricketers who played for Somerset in the vacation, and who was to take 500 wickets in his career at the expense of some of the most prolific batsmen of his age, was to encounter the gent whose bubbling humour was always to the fore in the Essex camp, Charlie McGahey. To quote from

R. Robertson-Glasgow's *46 Not Out*, in a sequence from the match at the Parks:

> It was in my 3rd match, this time against Essex, that I received a nickname that stuck. C.P. McGahey, the Essex batsman, a tough but benevolent character, then in his 50th year, had reached the middle 20s in Essex second innings, when he missed one from me and was bowled. The cricketers' dressing-room in the Parks is subterranean, so that those in it can follow the match by hearsay only. When McGahey walked down to it it seemed his captain, Johnny Douglas, asked him. 'How were you out, Charlie?' To which came the answer. 'I was bowled by an old . . . . I thought was dead 2,000 years ago, called Robinson Crusoe.'

From that time onwards Raymond Robertson-Glasgow became Robinson Crusoe by his countless friends. He, like Charlie, was a warm, engaging character who attracted people wherever he went. One had only to cross the threshold of the pavilion to be aware of his presence; his infectious laugh and good sense of humour lit bonfires of goodwill. In his later years he became a prolific conversationalist and writer.

He would always remember the humorous joke that gave him his name, and he still remembered the dear, sweet old man who did the honour of naming him.

Charlie, for his part, was proud to recount the story. The many customers who came to 'The Three Blackbirds' were told the fascinating tale, and it was soon to buzz around the environs of Leyton and Leytonstone. They, no doubt, would have thought it was typical of the chap with the 'bucks fizz' humour, and that it was another yarn to add to the many others.

Charlie, always ready to include his friends and colleagues in any story he might recall, was quick to point out that he shared the famous stand with Jack Russell. They had put on some 50 runs between them when Charlie was bowled, and were well set to make a good score if Robertson-Glasgow's full pitched ball, which McGahey later described as a 'yorker', had not spread-eagled the bails.

The 1920 season was to see Charlie play some memorable games, and the match against Middlesex, in Plum Warner's last season, was no exception. The Middlesex side was to end up county champions in 1920, and the team won its last nine games of the season.

The match against Essex at Leyton was to be Middlesex' last defeat. Although the Leyton wicket had the reputation of being kind to batsmen, this was not to be the case on this occasion.

In the first innings Essex was simply skittled out by Durston, Lee and J.W. Hearne for 133. That is, all except the 'Two Macs' and 'Mr Extras'. Charlie made 44 and Colin McIver 43, extras providing 25; the other nine batsmen could only raise 21 between them. The next best score was Perrin, who made 8. Charlie and McIver shared in a 6th wicket partnership of 70; 10 leg-byes and 15 byes were registered, indicating the spark in the wicket on the opening morning.

Middlesex ended their 1st innings 79 runs ahead. It was certainly an unusual second day as both Warner and Douglas had to attend a selection meeting at Lord's. Warner had to retire on 22 to make the journey, and Douglas left the field after bowling only 4 overs for the same reason. Warner's departure seemed to have an effect on both Hendren and Mann, as they were out soon after.

The Essex batting was a little more positive in the 2nd innings but this match was never going to be a high scoring game. Hearne finished with figures of 8–49, whilst only Perrin with 50, and Douglas 36 made any sort of contribution for Essex.

Although the wicket was not good, it was better than it was at the start of play, as Middlesex approached their second innings. Captain Douglas bowled superbly, 6–33 but, with 5 needed to win, Warner stood firm on 46 not out. It seemed a forgone conclusion, at this stage, that Middlesex would make the necessary deficit.

Just as all seemed lost for Essex the positive force of Douglas bowled a ball which pounded Warner. It was far too quick for his failing reflexes. The stumps were scuttled in all directions, and Essex were the victors by 4 runs. The team were ecstatic, whilst Charlie was thrilled, enjoying the season to the full.

The Middlesex match took place in July but there were other matches in this memorable season that were going to give Charlie much pleasure.

He and A.C. (Jack) Russell, going in first, knocked off the 102 needed to beat Northants in 80 minutes. Then Charlie and Bill

Reeves, whose combined ages totalled 94, made 121 for the 9th wicket against Worcester at Leyton.

The championship had, by this time, returned to a three day duration. This suited most players, and spectators as well, and Essex were equally happy with this situation. Charlie would have probably retired after the disastrous season of 1919 if it had not happened, even though after 1919 his matches were rather infrequent.

By 1921 Charlie McGahey was half a century old and it was time to bow out. Hard-hitting McGahey lacked the flair of Ranji, Fry or Jessop, but he was still a product of the Golden Age. He had learnt his cricket at that school, and the new school, with all its techniques, was too much to swallow at such a late age.

It was a year for much nostalgia and reflection, as many veterans neared the end of their careers. Korty, Lucas, and A.E. Russell had long since departed, and Carpenter finished his playing career in 1920. Fane, who started in 1895, had another year to go, whilst Percy Perrin soldiered on until 1928, lost, no doubt, without his twin.

1921 also saw the resignation of O.R. Borradaile, the Essex secretary. He had held the office for thirty years. Financial worries were ever apparent, and he did not always have an easy task. Prospects had fluctuated, and the temperaments of players had always to be taken into consideration. 'Borry' had soldiered on, and his efficiency helped Essex to overcome their many difficulties.

Sydney Pardon wrote in the *Wisden Almanack* of 1922: 'During all the years I have edited Wisden there has never been a season so disheartening as that of 1921.'

Cricket would only improve if 'young blood' was introduced into the game. It was a time for a new set of players to occupy centre-stage. Jack O'Connor began a career in 1921 which was to last until the start of the 2nd World War, while Hubert Ashton was also a 'new boy' in 1921. Laurie Eastman had begun a year earlier, and in the next few years the Essex team was to have many new faces.

As for Charlie, the time had come to reassess his life and his career. It was a time to take on new challenges and meet new demands, as well as the time to face up to life without participating in a sport which had been his life since a young lad. It was not good-bye but au-revoir. He may have been Middlesex born, but his heart was in Essex, and it was not to be too long before his warm and engaging personality once again would make its mark on Essex cricket.

9

Home is where the Heart is

In 1894, Leyton Cricket Club was a delightful little place opposite the Essex county enclosure. It had been rebuilt only two years before, and there was now a substantial fence erected all the way round with seating for a considerable number of people. There was also a new pavilion, and the wickets were perfect for first-class cricket, whilst soccer was played on the ground in winter to bring in extra revenue.

Charlie certainly enjoyed his time at the club, and would have agreed with the many people who considered it to be 'a good school' for the young cricketer. It gave him a good grounding in the game, and introduced him to players such as James Thorpe, a writer and cartoonist, who stated in his book *Cricket in a Bag* that Charlie was 'our best local product'.

The town had many notable occupants in its time; Pepys and John Evelyn both frequented the area in the 17th century, whilst Daniel Defoe was much impressed by the village when he came in 1722, and spoke of 'the handsome large houses with their many delightful coaches'.

When Charlie came to Leyton he came to a town which had soared in population over the preceding half-a-century. In 1850, the population of Leyton was only around 4,000, but by 1900 it had reached 75,000. Industrial London was spreading fast, and in 1874 a rail link was built to connect East London, including Leyton, to Ongar and the surrounding district.

Charlie was invited to lodge with Bill Golding, the then Chairman of Leyton CC, at his pub 'The Three Blackbirds', in Leyton High Road. This pub had been in the Golding family for many years. In fact Ann Golding had the inn in 1870. She had many children, but it was her son William, born in 1849, and commonly known as Bill, who was to take over the responsibility of running the premises on her death.

In 1892, Bill was quoted by *The Leytonstone Express & Independent* as 'hosting the annual dinner of Leyton CC in his "usual fine style", and presenting the awards in the club rooms of the public house'. He was a man of some standing in the town, and for some time now had allowed his premises to be used for committee meetings and the club's annual dinner.

The young McGahey soon settled down to life in Leyton. He gave Bill Golding a hand in the pub, and also did some paper work for the older gent. Golding had links with the town's soccer club as well, and Charlie's commercial experience came in handy to occupy his time when he was not on the sporting field, as well as to give him an income.

Although Charlie was playing for Essex CCC by 1893, he still managed to turn out for his club side, Leyton, on occasions when Essex did not have a game. In 1896 he was quite impressive. He amassed a total of 205 runs for the club against Clapton and, in all, made 499 runs. Quite a feat for a player who was not participating on a regular basis!

The following season saw him back with Leyton again and, in the June of that year, he turned out for the club against Clapton in a highly entertaining match in which Charles Kortright also participated.

A good crowd came to witness the event, which saw boundaries coming in quick succession once the two celebrities were together at the crease. Charlie made 41 before losing his wicket and, after his departure, the game was held up for Leyton Cricket Club to be photographed. Leyton finished on 180–7 and won the match by 54 runs.

As time passed, Charlie found less and less time to play for Leyton. London County, the Licensed Victuallers, and even Percy Perrin's club, Tottenham, took up much of his valuable time. But he never forsook the club that brought him to fame. Essex CCC and Leyton CC worked too closely together for that. Charlie, Percy Perrin and Charles Kortright often went over to the Leyton ground when Essex did not have a match, or on days when matches finished early, to coach the young players.

Before long, Charlie became a celebrity in Leyton and the surrounding district. Up-to-date news of his cricketing successes were quick to circulate, and he certainly attracted many visitors to The Three Blackbirds. Bill Golding must have been grateful to his young friend for the increased trade!

The local inhabitants loved to have this amateur soccer player, who later became one of the hardest-hitting batsmen of the Golden Age, in their midst, and were proud to call him 'their own'. Over the years they queued for his autograph, listened with amazement to his tales, worshipped his modesty and generosity, and missed him terribly when he deserted them and went up to Repton. Fortunately their despair was short-lived, and when in 1928 he returned to live in the area they rewarded him with the nickname 'Cheerful Charlie'.

By 1930 Bill Golding had died, and his son Bill had taken over as landlord of The Three Blackbirds public house. Bill Golding junior was not much younger than Charlie, and the two had been great pals over the years. Golding, like his father before, had connections with Essex CCC, and by this time was Vice-Chairman of the county, as well as being Chairman of Leyton Football Club.

He was, in Sonny Avery's words: 'A big, stout man with a jolly nature, who reminds one of a country farmer.' Sonny, who later excelled as such a great opening-batsman for Essex in the years prior to, and after, the 2nd World War, remembers winter nights in the pub with affection. 'I can often recall having steak and onion rings, a speciality of the pub, and seeing Charlie serving behind the bar', says the Essex cricketer.

Sonny Avery had connections with Leyton from as early as 1930. In that year he was employed by Essex CCC to work in the office at the county's headquarters. He progressed on to the ground staff, and admits he learnt much of his cricket in those early days by 'just observing others'.

The Essex cricketer was also a useful soccer player. He played for Ilford FC until the 1934–35 season when he was approached by the writer's father, Tom Cable, the then manager of Leyton Football Club, with a view to joining the Leyton side. Sonny has this to say about the meeting: 'Tom's charming manner and gentle persuasion won me over, and I moved to Leyton FC the following season. It was a move, incidentally, I never regretted.'

Tom Cable was born in Barking, on 27 November 1900, and

86

had a colourful football career which spanned from the end of the First World War until the early 1930s. He joined Spurs as a professional in 1928, and stayed on the club's books until 1932, when he followed his team-mate, Frank Osbourne, to Southampton.

However, it was as an amateur that he had most success. He played for Barking for a short time, and later QPR, before joining Leyton, a club which was to capture his heart.

Leyton Football Club was founded in 1889 and was known at that time as Matlock Swifts. The club was re-named Leyton in 1893. It competed in the South-East Essex League at the turn of the century, and before the First World War entertained teams in the London, Western and Eastern Essex Leagues. Later, the side returned to the South-East Essex League.

In 1921–22, the club re-joined the London League, winning the Championship three times, before joining the Athenian League in the 1927–28 season as holders of the Amateur Cup. Leyton won the Amateur Cup during Tom's third season with the club. It was the pinnacle of his playing career. Tom remembered the match well. Apparently it was a dirty, dismal day, and rain fell throughout the match. The pitch was covered with puddles as 12,684 people were assembled at Millwall's Ground, 'The Den', to see Leyton take on Barking Football Club.

The Barking team bought a wreath for him, which spurred him on to score a goal after only five minutes. Barking then equalized. But Salmons, who was also Barking born, went on to score for Leyton, giving them a good lead. Barking spent most of the second half fighting for the equalizer. This did not come. Tom clinched victory by scoring again. It was a 3–1 victory, and Leyton had won the Cup for the first time in its history. It was 9 April 1927.

The following year Leyton, once again, reached the final of the Amateur Cup. Middlesborough hosted the final at Ayresome Park on 14 April 1928. Cockfield was the team Leyton played, and Leyton fielded seven players from the previous cup winning side. 12,000 people turned out to watch this game.

Rutter gave Cockfield the lead after 14 minutes, but McKinley equalized for Leyton within a minute. Rutter, though, restored Cockfield's lead before half-time. Leyton equalized through Smith after 60 minutes, and Tom scored the winning goal 10 minutes from the end to enable Leyton to win the Cup.

Tom loved Leyton. It was like a second home to him. Many friendships were made with Essex cricketers of the time, including Jack Russell, Jack O'Connor, and the old goalkeeper, Stan Nichols.

Bill Krailing, a small, slight, cheeky chappy with twinkling blue eyes, kept 'The Coach & Horses', one of the many pubs in Leyton, and Tom and Bill would spend many happy hours together, pint in hand and soccer on the menu. But it was at The Three Blackbirds where Tom was most often to be seen, and it was there that he struck up a strong bond with Charlie McGahey.

Charlie would find a job in the office at Leyton Football Club during the winter months. Involved in a game he loved, he would also see a small sum of money for his efforts. Here he would work quite closely with Tom and, when not in the office, the two would meet at the pub. As Bill Golding was Chairman of Leyton Football Club, he would allow committee meetings to be held in the pub, and of course, Charlie was a permanent fixture behind the bar.

The pair shared an interest in soccer and cricket, and it was not surprising that they soon developed a certain rapport. They had both played for Tottenham Hotspur and both had kicked the ball on Millwall's ground. Tom often mentioned how pleased Charlie was to be present at the first Leyton Cup Final versus Barking at the 'Den'. It brought back memories of his old Millwall days, and he was happy to see the young Cable score the winning goal.

Although Tom turned professional in his late twenties, it was a decision he often regretted. He shared Charlie's view that amateur football was more enjoyable, less competitive in the ruthless sense, and certainly less commercial. It was a good experience for him to have a taste of professional life, but he was happy to return to the safe haven of amateurism.

Tom and Charlie shared many mutual friendships. During Tom's years at Southampton he met up with many players who represented Hampshire cricket, not the least of these being Johnny Arnold. Arnold was one of the few double Internationals, as well as being a fellow Southampton FC player. He was also the proud owner of a smart little MG sports car which was very good for Tom because Johnny would often take him up to London and call in at Leyton.

They would sometimes meet Charlie to have a chat and a few drinks. Often Laurie Evans was present and would join in the fun. Laurie looked after 'The Lion and Key', another Leyton pub, and Hampshire and other county teams stayed there whilst up at Leyton. The Essex lads always looked forward to the Hampshire team coming to town as much merry-making was made in very happy surroundings.

Charlie was famous for his reminiscences, and would hold the attention of many young players, Tom included. His tales of wondrous deeds achieved by the Essex team, in his younger days, seemed incredible. He would tell how Walter Mead took 17 wickets in a game against the Australians in 1893 for the loss of only 205 runs against his name. It seemed hardly possible. But it was true. The same man achieved it again in 1895, this time for 119 runs against Hampshire at Southampton. Only Freeman of Kent has equalled this feat.

Another remarkable match that Charlie liked to talk about was the one against the Aussies at Leyton in 1905. C.P. Buckenham 12–137 and Tremlin 8–135 took all 20 wickets, and Essex were the only county to beat the tourists that year. Charlie never let his audience forget this. It was the same with the Australian match of 1899 when The Cornstalks were skittled out for 73 in their 2nd innings. This was the lowest score of the tour.

The Golden Age seemed a life-time away. It was certainly another time. Charlie's recollections were 'little gems', Roy of the Rovers material which left the audience spell-bound.

Tom recalled how Charlie would make legendary W.G. Grace seem like a mythical God. His size; his power; his magnetism; they were all points to savour. The various tales of his gamesmanship and the episode with Ernest Jones, who bowled a ball through his beard were all so well expounded.

Charlie was always full of kind words concerning Charles Kortright, considered by many to be the fastest bowler of all time. He thought in 1896 that 'Korty' was 'even faster than Richardson, especially in the first dozen overs or so'. Kortright took 6 wickets in 12 balls against Surrey in 1895, and this took some doing, so it was no surprise that the younger generation listened with such eagerness.

Tom managed a pub in the East End of London for a time in his mid twenties. Through his friendship with Bill Golding and Bill Krailing he came to know the Webster brothers who owned a number of pubs around the area. One such pub was 'The Coach and Horses', which was managed by Bill Krailing, and another was 'The Royal Hotel' in Southend.

'The Ranleigh Arms' was another pub that came under their ownership and, when the pub became vacant of a landlord, Tom was approached to fill the position. Prior to this he was working on a part-time basis as a tally clerk in the London Docks, after leaving his job in the fur business, and returning from a highly enjoyable trip to Switzerland touring with the 'Middlesex Wanderers'.

The pub was situated at 'Ye Olde Forde', near Bromley-By-Bow. It was real cockney country, and most of the visitors to the pub were real cockney characters. A great many of them were costermongers who kept stalls in the colourful square which, in those days, was full of bright and beautiful flowers. There were clothes' as well as wares' stalls, and the first Caters food shop was situated near-by.

This was where the country folk from all around would bring their washing, and do a little shopping in this sort of mini market town. It is hard to believe that green fields and leafy lanes were only a 'stones throw' away from 'Old Bow'.

The Webster brothers bought pubs that were not a paying concern. Their aim was to build up a business before selling it. This was also the case with The Ranleigh Arms. After 18 months the pub was a bustling concern, and it had built up quite a trade. Tom had enjoyed his stay at the pub and had made many good acquaintances, but at the time the Websters' were considering selling the pub he was thinking of moving on to pastures new.

Charlie had been quite instrumental in attracting customers to The Ranleigh Arms. He helped out in the bar on occasions, and often, when Tom was away on cup-tie duty for QPR or Leyton, would step in as the reliable host. This was the area of Charlie's birth; ground that he was much familiar with, and it was always a certainty that the pub would be 'pretty full' when customers spread the word that Charlie was in town.

Often Charlie would liaise with other publicans. He would do some public relations work for Bill Golding, and was a familiar figure in not only Webster-run pubs, but in many hostelries throughout Essex. Tom had memories of coming down to Southend with Charlie, taking the tram up the High Street from the railway station and visiting 'The Railway Tavern', in Prittlewell. The publican was, needless to say, a friend to Charlie, and would have a meal waiting 'on the house'.

Charlie would like a 'Bass' or two and, wound-up in true fashion, would charm and entertain hosts and customers alike. There was no need for a comic in the house when this colourful character was present.

Visits to Leigh-on-Sea, the quaint little fishing village close to Southend, was another venue for Charlie and Tom. Although famous for its cockles and winkles, it also has numerous pubs, several of which were known to Charlie. The popular cricketer was certainly not lacking in friends, and many of these were wanting to hear about his playing days, his tours, and even his matches for the Licensed Victuallers, for whom he had turned out quite regularly.

The air at Leigh-on-Sea suited his health; the clean salty air cleared his chest, which was always a little suspect since his lung disease many years before. He would return to the grime of the East End, ready to face the evil polluted air; ready to inhale the smoke and fumes from the surrounding factories, a feature of life to which he was long accustomed.

Charlie was like a father-figure to Tom. Tom's own father had been a casualty of the First World War. Although he survived the initial drowning, caused when his boat was torpedoed whilst mine-sweeping off Malta, his health declined, and he did not live long after 'The Great War'.

Tom found Charlie a great comfort; full of support in times of trouble, and always ready to take a back seat when 'things were going well'. As Tom would say: 'This is the essence of the man: He was a great confidence builder: His warm and engaging manner touched the hearts of all those who knew him:'

According to Tom, 'Charlie always appreciated the advice and help he had in his younger days, and wanted to pass this on to others'. There were many older gents around when Charlie was a lad, not the least of these being Bill Golding senior, a valid friend and confidant, who took Charlie under his wing.

Golding was a man of firm ideals, but extremely fair. He stuck by Charlie even in those early days when Charlie was 'just a rough hitter', and helped Charlie to believe in himself. He instilled confidence in the young McGahey allowing him to take account of his failings, and improve upon them where necessary. He regarded Charlie like a son, a fact that Charlie much appreciated and never forgot.

Charlie had, by Xmas 1934, left his lodgings at the Three Blackbirds and found accommodation with a Scottish lady, in Queens Road, Leytonstone. It is not known exactly why he moved out, but it did coincide with Bill Golding's marriage to a fellow publican who had three daughters by a previous marriage. The great friendship formed over the years between Charlie and Bill had soured. Perhaps, also, there was a certain amount of jealousy on Bill Golding's part, especially as Bill's father held Charlie in such high esteem. Although greatly saddened by the move initially, Charlie settled down well to life with the elderly lady, who cared and catered for him admirably in his final years.

The Festive season, perhaps, did not have the same meaning to Charlie as it did to most family men. He had not married, and had, by this time, only brother Sydney as his kin. Sydney, eight years his senior, had been widowed for thirteen years, and lived in retirement with his housekeeper in Forest Gate. He had been a railway clerk during his working years, and unlike Charlie had ventured little from his life and work in London's East End.

It appears, from Tom, that Charlie's nomadic existence, with little care for routine or stability, contradicted strongly with the ideals impressed on him by his family. Their strict and staid middle-class traditions believed one should settle for a steady life and, although they were proud of his athletic achievements, they had very little to do with him him after he moved to Leyton. If Charlie minded this fact he certainly did not show it; he had his friends, and they were excellent company for him, providing much comfort and support at all times.

The rotund, jovial, Laurie Evans, had been a friend to Charlie for many years, and the two became even closer after the rift erupted between Charlie and Bill Golding. 'The Lion and Key', a corner pub near the pretty old church, St Mary with St. Edward, was quite a distance from Charlie's old lodging house, so it was not surprising that Charlie was such a frequent visitor.

It was taken for granted that Charlie would call in for a few drinks on that fateful Xmas and, by all accounts, he was in very good spirits when he left the pub that day. It appears, he just slipped and fell and, pulling himself together, managed to stagger to his lodgings.

On his arrival home, he went to bed, falling into a deep sleep almost immediately. He probably had a fair amount to drink, and was unaware of the seriousness of the cut to his finger. When his landlady failed to rouse him, she realized something was seriously wrong, and called a doctor. Charlie was then rushed to Whipps Cross Hospital in a critical condition.

Tom was at home in Barking that Xmas Day in 1934. Leyton did not have a fixture so Tom was not aware of Charlie's horrific accident. When he heard the following day, he was absolutely shattered. He had often spoken over the years of the suffering Charlie must have endured. The pain he had to contend with alone. 'Charlie would have been the first to offer assistance to others, and always the last to make a fuss himself.' Tom would recount. It was really a terrible tragedy!

Tom died in May 1986 following a massive stroke. His memory had faded over the years, and his mind was not so quick, nor so alert as it had been in earlier times. His memory of Charlie, though, did not recede; his recollections of him were as vivid as if it had all happened yesterday. It was hard to imagine that Charlie died fifty years before, and that Tom was only thirty-four years old at the time.

Only weeks before Tom died he could recollect the sound of the train rushing over the bridge behind The Blackbirds, and Charlie's familiar, warm, pleasant voice telling him it was time to climb the steps and board the last train for Barking. A drink in the bar, and a chat in 'the Birds' were an eternity away, but the magic of McGahey remained with him forever.

10

The Repton Connection

When many a cricketer retired from the first-class game he faced a major dilemma! What would he do next? Public approval no longer shone on him and he was back in the rat-race again, often facing boredom and relative obscurity.

Sometimes a player would resort to pints of ale at the end of the day. If alcohol became a habit it might take its toll, and the unlucky participant could end his life in utter misery. The cricketer might lose his confidence altogether, and life away from the limelight could quite unhinge his mind.

Arthur Shrewsbury, the greatest professional batsman of his day, was a prime example. He shot himself in 1903 from sheer disbelief that his illness was curable.

Then there was the death, in 1914, of A.E. Trott, the Australian and Middlesex cricketer. He was only forty-two years old and had been an in-patient at St Mary's Hospital, London, for over three years. Soon after leaving that institution he was found dead in bed by his landlady; a Browning pistol by his side. His great years were 1899 and 1900 when he achieved the feat of taking over 200 wickets and making 1,000 runs.

The suicide of the great A.E. Stoddart was another sad event a year later. He captained England at both 'rugger' and cricket, but it was as a batsman that he was most famous. Stoddart scored fast in the old-fashioned attacking style, and yet, had quite a sound defence. He could hit balls of all paces and all lengths, and he dearly loved a duel with a fast bowler.

Stoddart had given up the secretaryship of Queen's Club the previous year on account of bad health and a nervous breakdown. He had done nothing since, and was in financial difficulties as he had lost all his money through the War. This played on his mind, and he became another victim of the 'bullet wound'.

8. The playing fields of Repton.

Not all cricketers, though, were unable to cope after their playing days were over. Many of them looked forward to treading a new path. 'Plum' Warner became a prolific writer, as did E.H.D. Sewell, the old Essex player; others became Army Officers, or went to work in the City, whilst many became schoolmasters or professional coaches.

Claude Percival Buckenham had played 258 matches for Essex between 1899–1914 and toured South Africa with the MCC in 1909–1910. He was regarded as one of the deadliest fast bowlers of his time, taking 100 wickets in a season six times. Coaching seemed a natural progression from the first-class game, and when Len Braund left his post as professional coach at Repton in the summer of 1921, Buckenham took up the position.

He came to a school which was going through 'a bad patch' in cricketing terms. There had been little achievement since 'The Great War', and this was a period for rebuilding.

In 1922 the bowling was weak, but the side could bat down to number 10 and the fielding was beginning to improve. Players such as N.C.E. Ashton, A.C.J. German, E.K.M. Hilleary and H.W. Baines were beginning to show their worth, and the school managed to beat Shrewsbury, whilst having even draws with both Uppingham and Malvern.

After one season Buckenham decided that life at the public school was not for him. Perhaps the rigours of coaching were too intense; one had to have a great deal of patience and tolerance for this demanding job, as well as allowing for the fact that life was quieter at the school, away from public acclaim.

Repton needed a professional coach who was prepared to stay for a number of years: someone who would have a good rapport with staff and boys alike, and who would instil confidence in those young lads who had the potential to grow to maturity as schoolboy players.

Charlie McGahey was just the character needed to fill the vacant position. As Percy Perrin said of his great twin: 'Charlie was one of the most popular and kindest hearted players ever seen in first-class cricket. Certainly, he was most encouraging to any young player. I have known him on many occasions go out of his way to give a youngster good advice.'

These attributes did not leave Charlie once his playing days

96

were over and, if any player was suited to coaching, it must have been the 'likeable' McGahey. He was not one to sulk because he could participate no longer in the game he loved. He had enjoyed a long and skilful career, and he wanted to pass on any advice he could to the younger generation. He remembered with fondness his past, but he did not dwell on it to a point where it would cause depression, and his ability to take life in its stride had its advantages. He was very adaptable and, unlike many retired cricketers, did not mind taking a background role.

So Charlie became professional coach at Repton School in 1923, and another chapter in his life was beginning. On the train journey from Leyton up to Derbyshire he must have been pensive in thought; always a sentimentalist, he would be settling at a school where many of his contemporaries were educated.

C.B. Fry was probably Repton's most famous pupil. Stiff and awkward when at school, Fry developed in later years into a good all-round sportsman. The majesty of his cricket is so well documented, but he was also a notable Corinthian footballer who, in 1901, was capped for England against Ireland, as well as being a very powerful athlete. Charlie would have had many confrontations with him over the years on the cricket field.

Lionel Palairet was another 'old boy' who was at his best when he had left the Public School. The tall and handsome Palairet had all the shots, and records show he scored not only with effortless ease, but at a pace which would amaze modern players. Charlie, like others of his age, would have thought of him as dignified, and incapable of anything but elegance in any movement he tackled, be it dancing or lawn tennis.

As Charlie's journey progressed, his train of thought probably wandered from one aspect to another. He must have realized that his job was to be hard and sometimes tiring; more often than not he would be trying to teach and train boys who were, perhaps, not eager to learn. Many schoolboys would, perhaps, go through the motions with very little interest in the matter at hand.

This made coaching very difficult and must have depressed many men. Charlie would hardly have been dejected by this. The thought of producing a Fry or a Palairet would have spurred him on and fired him with excitement.

Some players that Charlie had played against during his years with Essex had excelled as schoolboy cricketers whilst at Repton.

J.N. Crawford was a Surrey player of some note in his time, and in the vacation of 1904 played for the county, taking 44 wickets at 16 runs apiece. He made 54 in his debut in first-class cricket against a very strong Kent side, which was immensely strong in the bowling department.

He was not yet 19 when, in the winter of 1905, he went with H.D.G. Leveson-Gower's side to South Africa, making 1,000 runs and taking 100 wickets. In 1907-08 he took 30 wickets in the 5 Test Matches played by A.O. Jones' XI in Australia. The great Clem Hill rated him as the greatest all-round player he had seen on Australian soil; amazingly Crawford played in spectacles, always an awesome task. F.R.D.O. Monro said of Crawford in his book on *Repton Cricket:*

> J.N. Crawford was definitely the greatest Reptonian and probably the only schoolboy cricketer capable even at 17 of winning any school match single handedly. He had immense maturity as an all-round cricketer even at that tender age. A powerful bat whose attack was based on a fundamentally sound technique, this accompanied a good medium pace action which saw results for its accuracy. He was a fine field and captained Repton in 1905.

In the eyes of Alfred Cochrane, J. Howell was the most outstanding player before the War years. Cochraine says of him:

> It is doubtful if we have ever had a better batsman at Repton than John Howell was during his last 2 seasons. Crawford and Francis Ford were more powerful and brilliant but they were not more difficult to get out. Fry and Palairet were at their best some years after they had left school, and of that company of fine players who, a few seasons ago, won matches under Altham's captaincy there was not one who individually could compare with Howell as he was in 1913 and 1914 . . . long innings . . . were characteristic of him, Howell could go on hour after hour with the machine-like accuracy of a first-rate professional.
>
> Such proficiency requires certain qualities of concentration, as well as the power to recognize your own limitations. When he was in form it was hopeless to bowl at him and no player of his years gave his innings away less often.

During the four seasons he was in the XI, Howell went in 14 times in the matches against Malvern and Uppingham, and never once failed to reach double figures. His total runs in these engagements amounted to 690, which gives him the average of almost 49. He was generally acknowledged to be the best schoolboy bat of the year and moreover was a good captain and judge of the game.

None of those who played against him could doubt that, had he lived longer, he would have been going in first for England very soon after he left school. Unfortunately, this was not to be. He was killed in action in September 1915.

Repton holds the memory of John Howell close to its heart. It has named the tea room in the pavilion after him, and the best player each season is still presented with 'The John Howell Bat'.

As Charlie pondered further, his mind must have concentrated on various men he remembered during his playing career. W.R. Murdoch, son of Billy, the old Australian captain, had been at Repton, as had W.L. Price, who later played for Worcestershire. He also appeared for Canada and the USA in 1912. Then, there was the keen Altham, who became a good player for both Surrey and Hampshire, W.T. Greswell, of Somerset, and J.S.L. Vidler of Sussex. Such pleasant memories had abounded and Charlie must have been at home before he arrived.

There must have been certain reservations. Charlie would have wondered if the years in the doldrums since the war would continue. He must have thought about the time ahead, and about the young boys who waited to be nursed and tendered to maturity.

Would there be any boys with the qualities of past greats? Hopefully none were to be plucked from us in their prime like the great Howell! Only time would tell what lay ahead. So on his arrival at Repton he prepared for one of the greatest challenges of his life.

Charlie came to a school which in the mid-1840s had only a handful of pupils and little facilities for sport. By 1866 there were around 200 boys at Repton and clearly something had to be done to arrange playing fields for organized games.

Over the years 'The Monks' Paddock' was added to the original ground and levelling and draining were carried out all over the lower field, whilst 'The Doctors' Paddock', at the northern end, was included in 1884. The cricket field at Repton is well described in F.R.D.O. Monro's book *Repton Cricket*.

> Repton now possess a grand 7 acre field. Strangely enough, considering its marshy origin, it is comparatively dry and recovers quickly from rain – a testimony to the efficiency of the drainage system. Beyond careful top dressing the turf requires little attention and the wickets are good.
>
> Before the introduction of summer-time, batting during the last critical hour was made more exciting by the shadow of the church spire which fell directly across the pitch. That problem no longer exists, and the light is generally very good, though ageing cricketers fielding or (fumbling) by the sheds sometimes complain that the background of the school buildings make it difficult to sight the ball – but take it in all, no school could wish for a better, more delightful ground on which to play cricket.

Repton certainly has its charm and must have been an excellent haven for the retired cricketer. The public school, originally a grammar school, was founded in the 16th century and preserves part of an ancient priory, whilst the 17th-century Hall now serves as the headmaster's house. This 'old worldly' paradise is set in the lovely county of Derbyshire, with its lush green valleys and magnificent rolling hills, and the school has long had links with the county side.

John Louis Crommelin-Brown was born in Delhi, India, in 1888, and after school in Winchester, and a game in the Freshman's Match at Cambridge, went to Derbyshire as a good middle-order right-hand batsman. From 1921 he became master-in-charge at Repton School. The professional was employed for the summer term only, and was there to aid the master, who was really in charge of coaching.

According to C.J. Wilson, one of the best leg-break bowlers of the time at Repton, Charlie's job was not an easy one: The professional was very much second fiddle and had to obey the rules of coaching laid down by the master. Mr Wilson goes on to say: 'It must have been very galling for Charlie as he was a much older man and a more experienced player than Crommelin-Brown.'

Charlie, though, was in his 50s now, and although it was

correct to say he had played a great deal longer than his master-in-charge, he was probably quite content to take a background role. At his age it is highly unlikely that he would want to make many important decisions.

His hours of work were probably from 2.30pm–6pm on half-holidays. Half-holidays occurred 2 or 3 times a week. There was also net practice which would last for 1–2 hours. Fielding practice followed this twice a week for the first team and, often, a net bowler was employed. One of these was another remarkable man, Fred Tate, of England and Sussex, who was father of the great Maurice.

Fred Tate was born in 1867 in Brighton and played in 312 matches for Sussex between 1887-1905. He was a good all-rounder whose one test match in 1902 saw him being chosen on the morning of the first day in place of G.H. Hirst. Tate went in to bat as England's last man with 8 runs needed for victory. He was dismissed for 4 and England lost by 3 runs. Significantly, he took 100 wickets in a season five times, and his best figures were 9–73 for Sussex versus Leicester at Leicester in 1902. Charlie would have met him on many occasions.

J.W. Buckland, a good batsman of the time and one of the best slip fielders the school has ever had, was in the Repton XI from 1923–25. Although now around eighty years of age, he remembers his old coach with affection, and says:

> I can picture him as a heavily built man with a lovely jolly character, and a very happy disposition. He was a good coach and always very good fun.

Charlie obviously left a lasting impression on this quick scoring batsman who was at his most effective on fast pitches. He would have taken pride in a player such as Buckland, as he entered the XI in the first year that Charlie was coach. Charlie must have felt he had some part to play in making him such a fine player.

The opening pair of B.H. Valentine and H.W. Austin were to prove most useful additions to the team in the mid-1920s. Austin, it is felt, would have become first-class if it had not been for the demands of lawn tennis, and Valentine was to go on to become a brilliant captain for Kent in the mid 1930s.

According to Jack Mendl, a most accomplished player who first played in the XI in 1928: 'It is generally regarded that they would have done equally well in each others' sport.' In fact the pair won the Doubles Public School Lawn Tennis Championship in 1925.

'Bunny' Austin remembers making 0 in his first innings for Repton, but in his last match for the School against Malvern in 1926 scoring a fine 102 not out. His recollections of Charlie are of Charlie's insistence on 'high catches'.

Of course, fielding on the boundary for so many years to bowlers such as Charles Kortright would have impressed on the 'old professional' the need for long, high throws. It would be pleasing to think that Charlie had a part to play in making Bunny such a fine ball player.

Bunny was a finalist in the 'Wimbledon Singles' event in 1932 and 1938, and appeared as a semi-finalist in the 'Doubles' events on numerous occasions in the years leading up to the 2nd World War.

If one had to pick a 'star' batsman of these years, it would have to be Bryan Valentine. Monro says of him in his book on *Repton Cricket:* 'He was a brilliant bat with most of the cricket scoring strokes, and when disposed of, it was generally through over eagerness.' It was not long before his skills were discovered by Kent; he started playing for them in 1927, and by the early 1930s was a firmly established member of the side.

Valentine would have seen his 'old coach' occasionally when Kent took on Essex in the County Championship. Charlie, then Essex scorer, would have, no doubt, taken great delight in seeing how his young protege had blossomed. Like Charlie's connections with the Essex club, Valentine was for all his life attached to Kent. He was President in 1967, and this very cheery chap attended Kent matches up until his death in 1983.

1923 was a fair year for Repton cricket, 1924, quite good, whilst 1925 was a 'really good year', the best the school had had for some time.

Austin made 475 runs in 14 innings, and Buckland also did well with the bat, scoring 502 runs in 12 completed innings. Valentine played brilliantly. He made a chanceless 115 against Uppingham and a very bright 119 against the Pilgrims; in all he made 592 runs. These three players were responsible for 70 per cent of the runs made, even though Rennick and R.H.C. Human played some valuable innings.

The bowling, meanwhile, was strong. Rennick, when not handicapped by strains, bowled fast and well. Piper and Sharpley were good support, as was C.J. Wilson, whose first year in the XI this was.

By 1926 Charlie was an established personality at the school. He was mid-way through his spell at Repton now, and must take some credit for the way the team was performing. C.J. Wilson remembers that it was around this time that the lads began to have confidence in Charlie.

Mr Wilson recalls: 'It took us a while to get used to this big man, as I remember him, with a dry sense of humour to which we were not accustomed. We did not see Charlie other than at practice, in the nets, or at matches, which meant that it took quite some time for his character to impress itself on us boys. But it did, and in 1926 we paid a lot of attention to what he told us.'

'I liked him a great deal,' he goes on to say. 'When he began to reminisce he would always preface any statement with the words, "I sat down", something the boys found most amusing. One of his tales, I remember, was of his captaining the MCC side in Australia against a local team in the outback. When tossing for who was to bat first and losing said "One to you: In England we always toss best of 3." '

Another old Reptonian who was in the Repton XI in 1926 was A.J. McAlpine. Mr McAlpine also had very good memories of Charlie and found him very encouraging and extremely cheerful. 'I certainly feel he brought on the cricket very well and did help me a great deal in my cricketing career.' McAlpine made some reasonable scores this season.

Reggie Hewetson, now General Sir Reginald Hackett-Hewetson, remembers being coached by Charlie for three years and has recollections of him as 'a lovely man, so kind and generous'. The General played in the first team in 1926 and helped the school on a damp wicket, to register a fine win against Uppingham School.

By 1928, Repton had one of the best fielding sides ever. The two Humans, Joyce, Clark and Oldfield added to the very strong line-up, as did another remarkable batsman, Jack Mendl.

The latter had quite a colourful career in cricket. He made 173 for Repton against Leicester Gents in 1927 which was his first match for the public school. It gave him great pleasure, as did his 213 for Oxfordshire versus Devonshire twenty-two years later. A good right-hand batsman he represented Scotland and MCC in his time whilst in later years he became an excellent coach.

Mr Mendl has very pleasant memories of his 'old coach' and remembers him with affection. 'He was a friendly and helpful coach and although in his mid-50s, a very good net bowler. I was very sorry I did not see him play in his heyday.' A story the pupil remembers concerns a match when Repton were playing Shrewsbury in 1928:

> Charlie was given the job by our master-in-charge of sending telegrams to Repton giving details of the match as it progressed. This meant going to the nearest GPO via a toll-bridge and, I believe a local hostelry. Charlie sent off the telegrams during each interval and had to pay the toll each time. Eventually he became fed-up with paying up. On the final occasion, when we were heading back to Repton, we heard our professional shouting at the toll-keeper. 'How much will I have to pay to buy your b. . . . . bridge?' I seem to remember we had to assist our very popular pro back into the taxi and subsequently on to the train.

It appears, according to one famous pupil, that the lads nipped off to the nearest pub for a drink if there was no-one around to notice. Although there is no mention of Charlie's presence at these meetings, it is highly likely that he was there. If a drink was on the cards Charlie was not backward in coming forward, and it may be that he was even an instigator in the matter. If so, it must have been a terrible shock to the pupils when he decided to part company with the school.

He had taken delight, over the years, viewing the banks of the ruins looking across to the sheds with the noble elm standing over them. He had experienced drowsy afternoons with windows open wide, and had witnessed the stately umpires walking to the wicket, whilst the schoolboys sat on deck-chairs with cherries at hand, ready to view the annual Malvern or Uppingham match.

The memories of burnt-out Junes' would be clear in his mind, and would have revived in his thoughts whenever he passed under the arch, or spied the spire above, but after 1928 these delights were to be only memories. 1929 was to produce the best school team since 1925 but Charlie was not there to see it!

His years at the school had provided good experience for the professional coach and he, no doubt, enjoyed them immensely, but now he had been offered a position as coach to the Essex side. This was a chance to come back to the county for whom he had scored so many runs in the past, and the club for whom he held so much affection.

He would be able to help and train Essex youngsters, and would have more of a free hand in displaying his talents. It was the end of Repton cricket for him, but he would not forget the many friendships he had made, and his time at the school certainly was a very enjoyable and highly fruitful period in his life.

11

A Great Encourager

Quite a change had taken place on the Essex county cricket scene whilst Charlie was tucked away at Repton! The ground at Leyton had been a financial worry to the club ever since they bought it, and now there were mortgages amounting to £10,000.

The committee felt the future of the county would be assured if these could be wiped out. With this in mind, long negotiations took place in 1922 with the Army Sports Board, with a view to selling the Leyton Ground. An amicable arrangement was reached, and the Army allowed Essex to use the Leyton ground for most of their home fixtures.

Although the sale of the ground aided the finances for a time, and, from 15th place in 1921, Essex rose to 8th in 1923, membership was not too good. By 1924, Essex were again facing a financial crisis, and made an appeal for funds from the public for £1,000.

Quite a few county clubs were in similar financial difficulties, and, at a time when many football clubs were going to the wall, the supporters of cricket clubs would always show great loyalty and seem ready to bale out the 'strugglers'. The public responded well to the cry for help, as did the players, who rewarded their admirers by reaching 7th position in the championship in 1925.

'Jack' Russell was, by this time, firmly established as a leading batsman in the side. He was to make 71 hundreds in an outstanding career. Jack O'Connor, another batsman of England calibre, was also scoring admirably; then there was the sparkling all-rounder, Laurie Eastman, and Stan Nichols, who was to achieve 'The Double' eight times between 1929 and 1939. Leonard Crawley, who made a fine 176 not out to give Essex a fine victory over Sussex in 1927, and the brilliant Hubert Ashton, could only play on limited occasions, but they managed to add lustre and variety to the XI when they did make the side.

The bowling strength was quite weak. The exception was the brilliant, J.W.H.T. Douglas, but Essex tended to rely too heavily on him. It was only on the occasions when G.M. Louden was present that his load was lightened a little. An appendicitis operation in the winter of 1925 took its toll on Douglas, and he could not re-join the Essex side until July 1926. His form, from then on, was quite disappointing, and it was becoming apparent that 'the great man' was past his best.

Charlie returned to a side which, in 1927, finished 8th in the championship. He was to spend two seasons as coach to the Essex side and, during those two seasons, a great deal was to happen. Many new players were to come under his wing and, with his kind, gentle manner, he was to guide them to maturity.

D.R. Wilcox began his career in 1928, and was later to become county captain, managing, like quite a few cricketers from the Universities, to combine a career in county cricket with school-mastering. Tom Wade first played for the club in 1929, and between then and 1950 scored a good 4,972 runs, whilst C.J.M. Watts, the old Reptonian, spent a brief time with Essex in 1928. He managed to score 119 runs in 11 innings. A fine forceful bat, he was at his best in a crisis, as his 145 for Repton against Malvern School showed in 1924. He possibly joined Essex on Charlie's recommendation.

The most colourful character of those years must have been the diminutive Roy Sheffield. His first game for Essex was in 1929, and his last, in 1936. He made 3,822 runs in his career, although it was as a very able wicket-keeper that he will best be remembered.

Tom Cable had recollections of several humorous outings with Roy. 'One afternoon,' Tom relates, 'Roy and myself were attending a cinema matinee and Roy insisted upon throwing the sweets that Mrs Sheffield had given us at the audience below. His aim was superb, attacking a poor, defenceless bald man a few rows in front of us. Eventually, the inevitable happened. He was asked to leave and myself with him.'

'On another occasion,' Tom continues, 'Roy was giving me a lift to Leyton in his Citroen car. As we were approaching Seven Kings, near Ilford, a highly congested area, trams were coming from all angles. Suddenly, Roy began to take his eyes off the wheel and started fiddling with his feet. He asked me to take the wheel, and there was I unable to drive. I had always been a motor-cycle rider. Luckily, he stopped playing around just in time.'

Roy Sheffield was born in Barking, Essex, in 1905, where his family had a Pawnbroker's shop. Tom knew both Roy and step-brother Alf quite well, and shared Roy's love of cricket and soccer. Roy played in goal for Barking, and remembers playing against Tom when he played for Leyton. In fact, the match in question was a cup-tie, and Leyton beat Barking in this local derby.

Roy also has fond memories of Charlie. Now living in New Zealand, this 'highly spirited' eighty-two year old tells how he found Charlie 'a gentle old chap'. On hearing I was writing this biography Roy said: 'Be kind to him, he deserves it. For the only person he ever harmed was himself.'

Apart from players who did make the first-team Charlie also encountered those who did not. The most notable of these must have been Alf Gover, the England and Surrey bowler, who in his own words 'nearly played for Essex'.

Alf Gover was aged eighteen at the time and was learning the business of building surveying. His annual holiday was about to start and a colleague in the office inquired as to his 'time-off plans'. He told his colleague that he would like to take in some cricket, and the colleague, who was a member of Essex CCC, told him in reply that he may be able to get him some club games. A trial was arranged at the Essex nets at Leyton and Alf Gover duly turned up at the appointed time, early on the first day of a county match. He was dispatched to the nets and told to bowl at a batsman who was just about to take guard. Alf Gover recalls the story in the *Cricketer:*

> It was not just a case of running a few paces and turning my arm over, but hurling the ball as fast as I could possibly manage. The nets' pitch being slightly worn, I hit the batsman several times on the gloves or the body in a hectic 15 minute spell. At the finish the batsman addressed a tall, burly man who had been watching my efforts, and in a curt tone of voice said: I'll see this boy in my dressing-room, Charles. Charles later transpired to be Charles McGahey, the Essex coach.

In my subsequent talk with Charles McGahey I found that my office friend had recommended me for a trial as a fast bowler forgetting to tell them I was simply looking for some holiday cricket. So off I went with the glad news to my parents, telling them I would have to stay in digs in the Leyton area.

Alf Gover stayed on the Essex staff until the following season when, after a meeting with Herbert Strudwick, who was the then Surrey scorer, he realized he could join Surrey as they desperately needed a first-team bowler. The rest, as we know, is history. It was certainly Essex' loss and Surrey's gain.

As always Charlie had his fellow man at heart, and I am sure he would have been most happy if he knew the young man of eighteen he coached would not only turn out to represent England, but would one day have his own coaching school. Alf Gover has been able to pass on the support and encouragement he had as a youngster to the many lads that have passed his way, and many cricketers over the years have been grateful for it.

The Surrey International has very good recollections, even today, of his 'old coach' at Essex. He recalls: 'My recollection of Charles was of a very kindly man who gave me every encouragement when I was under him as a young professional with Essex, and who was most understanding when I left Essex to join Surrey.'

It was during Charlie's years as coach that J.W.H.T. Douglas fell from favour and died in such tragic circumstances. 1928 was a disastrous season, from 8th position in 1927, Essex fell to 16th place in the Championship table and, as often happens when a sudden decline in form sets in, the job of captain was on the block.

The committee asked Douglas to resign, and then appointed H.M. Morris in his place. Disappointed and distressed, Douglas' life was to take its final tragic twist. He was drowned when the steamer in which he was sailing, was in a collision in thick fog in the Kattegat. He could have saved himself, but he went below to rescue his father and neither were seen again.

The years that Charlie coached Essex were short and sweet and not without incident. Nearly sixty years of age, he was feeling it was time to participate in a more restful form of occupation. He still had his patience and he still had his love for the game. When the job of scorer became vacant he jumped at it, and the final chapter of his colourful career unfolded.

12

A Scorer's Lot

For years the job of scorer has been undertaken by either retired players or retired club members. Many official county scorers' served their apprenticeship with the second XI, but this is by no means as complicated, or as involved, as first-team scoring. With a first-team match all the scores, averages, run rates and over rates have to be worked out and sent up to Lord's. So there is much more work than just recording details.

Charlie McGahey took on this complex but highly enjoyable position at the very late age of fifty-nine. Most people of his age were looking forward to 'taking things easy', but Charlie had spent all his savings and it was necessary for him to work. There was no retirement pension nor supplementary benefit; not that Charlie would have wanted such payments if they had been on offer. He was a proud man, and of the 'old school' where such benefits were considered charity. He had the necessary attributes for team-scorer, such as a flair for figures and an ability to concentrate on the game he loved, and in 1930 he set about the task in earnest.

Although each county had its own scorer who travelled around with the team, and although the scorers are usually old players, the scoring-box has always been neutral, and, even a visitor to the box, if he begins to take sides, is politely told to 'keep quiet'. Charlie would certainly not take sides, as Alf Gover points out: 'I often saw Charles when he was team scorer for Essex and I was playing for Surrey, and he would always pat me on the back if I took a few wickets.'

It must have been interesting for Charlie to see the game from another angle. As Herbert Strudwick, one time scorer for Surrey CCC noted in an article in *The Times* in May 1937: 'Scorers see more of the game than any spectator, and they should become

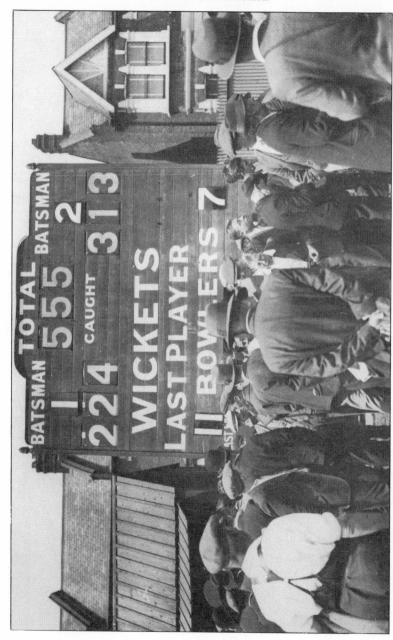

9. *The Essex scoreboard showing the controversial 555 total. June 1932.*

good judges of a player, for we have to watch every ball bowled, and to know every fieldsman and where he is fielding. Above all we have to keep our eye on the umpire because he is dictator of every run that is recorded – indicating how the runs should be put down by a series of signs.'

The score and analysis is totalled up at the fall of each wicket to see if they balance. The scores are then sent down to the printers, whilst the scorers answer any questions the representatives of the press might wish to hurl at them. If a player was new to the side they may wish to know his life story. All this had to be given whilst account had to be taken of the incoming batsman. Charlie soon learnt that he had to have his wits about him, as everything happened so quickly from the scorers box.

Charlie probably took all this in his stride, as Roy Sheffield points out: 'Charlie was never flustered. He adapted to his new life quite quickly, happy in the congenial atmosphere that surrounded the Essex camp.'

Fun and laughter were the order of the day at Leyton, in the last few years before it was abandoned as the official headquarters of Essex CCC. Brian Castor was the popular secretary in those days, and the team would take great delight in playing many tricks on him. He would often start a letter on his typewriter then disappear on business. In the meantime someone would step in and put something ridiculous in the letter. Brian on his return would realize what had happened and the inquisition would start. Apparently, Brian would take it all in good spirit!

A curious feature of Leyton's ground was the bell which warned people that play was about to commence. It was in a sort of belfry; its rope hanging from the ceiling. A favourite joke was to tie a rope high up in the ceiling, which could be done by standing on someone's shoulders. Then the secretary would be heralded and told it was time to ring the bell, and one would witness the language flow.

Even the introverted Percy Perrin realized the situation and fully enjoyed the flavour of Essex cricket in his retirement days as Charles Bray recounts:

> I was sitting with Perrin on the balcony of the pavilion at Leyton one lovely summer's day when Essex were batting.

The rest of the team were sporting themselves on the benches with the exception of the two batsmen. Each one had at least one girlfriend, some two. The boys had taken a bit of care over their appearance. Hair was gleaming in the sunshine: shirts shone: flannels were white and well pressed: Perrin looked at them for quite a time then turned to me and growled: 'Look, Charles, If we could perform in the championship as well as we court, we'd win the blink'in championship, hands down.'

Charlie adored this fun-loving atmosphere, even more so when he joined up with his old pal, Bill Reeves. It had often been said what a card was Reeves! This comic had made 271 appearances for Essex between 1897-1921, his playing career coinciding somewhat with Charlie's, but by now he had turned his attention to umpiring and was one of the most notable umpires on the cricketing circuit. Reeves was respected, knowing the game backwards, but he was also known for his clownish behaviour. 'That concludes the entertainment for the day, gentlemen.' He was often heard to utter as he whisked off the bails at 6.30pm, following a day's play.

Travel was tiring, and could become very tedious if there was not someone around to brighten up proceedings. Reeves' humour would often come to light when he was up against quite serious and dignified beings who probably did not know what to make of the jovial umpire.

R.W.V. Robins of Middlesex was one such unfortunate gent who came under the scrutiny of the ex-player. On one occasion Robins had appealed several times in one over to Bill Reeves, with no apparent luck.

'Do you want your sweater, Mr Robins?' declared Reeves at the end of the over, offering him the Middlesex sweater with its badge of three savage-looking 'seaxes'. 'No I don't, and you know where you can stuff it,' came the gist of the none too gentlemanly reply. 'What!' said Bill, 'swords & all.'

Another time, Essex was playing Surrey at Leyton and Reeves was chosen to umpire the game. Percy Fender was at the crease and in fine fettle, a sure century looked to be on the cards. Suddenly Reeves gave Fender the signal to depart. Apparently, Fender could not believe it. In sheer disbelief he approached

Reeves. 'Excuse me, Mr Reeves, I am sure I cannot be out. Your decision is incorrect, surely!' 'Well, Mr Fender,' came the reply, 'you have a look in tomorrow's papers, and you will see the result for yourself.'

Essex, perhaps, did not take cricket as seriously as they should if they were to be in championship contention. But life was fun. For Charlie it was extremely relaxing after the physical strains imposed on him over the years. Although he had to be mentally alert, he thought he could take a background role now and leave it to others to make cricketing history. This was not to be the case for a brief moment in 1932; the carnival atmosphere was brushed aside, and Charlie was to find for himself a very special niche in the annals of the game.

Tired from a gruelling day in the field at the Oval the previous day, the Essex team, along with Charlie, assembled at Leyton one June day in 1932 to take on the might of a powerful Yorkshire side. It was a perfect batting wicket, as was per usual at Leyton, when Herbert Sutcliffe and Percy Holmes, the Yorkshire opening pair, came to the wicket. Almost immediately they set about destroying the Essex attack. Thirty-four years earlier, another Yorkshire opening pair, J.T. Brown and John Tunnicliffe had made a record stand of 554 for the first wicket, and if the record was ever to be broken it seemed only a pair such as the two at the wicket that day could possibly achieve it.

Obviously, as the runs piled up this was on their minds. As they watched a ragged Essex team leave the field that day they could congratulate themselves on the fact that the only difficult chance they had of losing a wicket was when Percy Holmes was missed behind the wicket by Roy Sheffield when he was on 3. Charles Bray, the unfortunate Essex captain that day, recalls the unhappy situation at the end of the first day:

> At the close of the first day when I knew both batsmen were out to break the record, for I overheard Sutcliffe talking about it to his partner, I decided that as I had to conserve the new ball for the next morning, I would make it as difficult as possible for the Yorkshire pair to score rapidly against my tired bowlers. I brought on Laurie Eastman, who could usually be relied upon to bowl an accurate length and direction. My instructions were to bowl at, or outside the

115

off-stump, and with his agreement, I packed the off-side having only one fielder on the on-side.

His first 3 balls were outside the leg-stump, and bang, bang, bang, went 3 boundaries. A normal field had to be set and with it more space for the batsmen to get runs. Eastman apologized to me at the end of the over, saying, the attack was 'bowled out'.

The weather was fine and sunny the next morning when Holmes and Sutcliffe continued their innings. There was great excitement around the ground as it was odds-on the first-wicket record would be broken. The cricket writers turned up in force as did nearly the entire folk of East London. According to the writer's father, Leyton had never been packed with so many people, especially as Essex were on the losing side of a situation once again.

The late Ernie Coleman, who had connections with Leyton Football Club, and followed Essex cricket with considerable passion until his death in 1988, remembered Charlie when he was scorer for the club. He tells also how he could not wait to leave Leyton County High School and rush to see the famous match after school on that first day.

He said: 'I can remember going into the pavilion after a day's play in 1932 and gaining Charlie McGahey's autograph, which I still have to this day. Weeks later I raced out of school as a lad of ten to see that memorable match. Yorkshire were 250 for 0 at that stage, with Holmes and Sutcliffe ending the day on 423. A boy in my form played truant the next morning and saw a new world record for the first wicket set up. I wish, on reflection, I had too!'

The crowd did not have to wait too long to witness the record they had all come to see. Before lunch the scoreboard reached the magic 555 and *The Times* had this to say about the event on 17 June 1932:

> At Leyton, at exactly 1pm yesterday, Sutcliffe, by hooking a short ball from Eastman to the boundary, broke, in partnership with Holmes, the record first-wicket stand set up by Brown and Tunnicliffe in 1898. Sutcliffe promptly got out to the next ball. But the excitement was not yet over. For as soon as AB Sellers had declared the innings closed and the players had reached the pavilion, the figures 555 on the scoreboard, which meant that the record had been broken,

116

were changed into 554, which meant it had only been equalled. It was not until half-an-hour later that the new record passed into cricket history.

The two batsmen posed before the scoreboard for the press photographers whilst the score was on 555, and poor Charlie was left with egg on his face, as a discrepancy, it seemed, definitely had occurred. Charles Bray recounts his story of events:

> At Leyton the scorers sat directly underneath the board, and it was not an unusual occurrence for the board to differ from the scorers' book, but it was a very worried Charles McGahey, the Essex scorer, who came to see me in the Essex dressing-room.
>
> The umpires maintained that a no-ball signalled by one of them had not been recorded. Would I agree to this extra run being added? There was no doubt in McGahey's mind that a run was being found on this occasion. What did I think about it? I told Charles that I thought the two batsmen had put up a magnificent performance and that it would be cruel luck if they were deprived of the honour of breaking the record owing to a mistake on the part of our scoreboard. If the scoreboard said a no-ball had been signalled and not recorded it was OK with me.

The Times continues its report:

> It would have been the cruellest ill-fortune had a mistake of one run on the scoreboard robbed the batsmen of the full fruits of their triumphs. For their respective innings were so consistently and unfailingly sound that the strokes which sent the ball to any direction, other than that which they intended, could be counted on the fingers of two hands.
>
> The pitch was, of course, perfect – the record could hardly have been broken had it not been – but the secret of Holmes and Sutcliffe success lay not in the pitch, nor in the shortcomings of the Essex bowling, but in their endurance, their unfailing patience, and their vast technical resources.

When everything was finally reduced to statistics, it appeared that Sutcliffe gave no chance, and hit one 6, one 5, and 33 4s, and that Holmes, who might have been caught at the wicket when he had made 3, hit 19 4s. Sutcliffe's 313 was his highest individual score, and it enabled him to reach his 1,000 runs for the season, but

Holmes had 6 times up until then exceeded the 224 he made in this innings.

Roy Sheffield remembers clearly Charlie coming in to lunch saying that he quit the scoreboard before the crowd tipped it over. 'With all the hubbub Charlie had no chance of working anything out after 555 came down and 554 went up,' says Sheffield. He continues: 'Charlie sadly needed liquid sustenance after that episode, that's for sure.' The Essex wicket-keeper rated Charlie 'an efficient scorer', but of course, mistakes can happen.

Apparently, according to Billy Ringrose, the Yorkshire scorer, 'the Essex scorer had held out against the no-ball I had in my book.' This handsome bowler, who had to fight to get into the Yorkshire team of the 1890s, would not budge, and it was up to Charlie to give in.

According to E.J. (Tiger) Smith, the England and Warwickshire professional, who from 1930 was on the list of umpires', 'no fiddling was involved'. He was adamant about this when in conversation about the issue with Robert Brooke, writer and co-founder of the Association of Cricket Statisticians.

Tom Pearce, now Essex President, had long been amused by the result of the lost run because as he recalls: 'Charlie was always getting the scoreboard boys to get him bottles of Bass. Of course there was always a time when he needed to visit the lavatory, and it must have been during one of these periods that the run went missing. However, Charlie was most upset about it!'

The result was a heavy defeat for Essex. From Yorkshire's 555 for 1 declared, (Sutcliffe 313 Holmes 224 n.o.) Essex could only make 78 (Verity taking 5–8, and Bowes 4–38). In their second innings Nichols was the highest scorer with 59 not out. In a total of 164, Verity taking 5–45 and Bowes 5–47, Yorkshire won by an innings and 313 runs.

It is amazing, as Holmes was reputed to be suffering from lumbago during the match. Holmes and Sutcliffe ended their partnership the following year when Holmes retired. But Sutcliffe, eight years younger than his partner, still had 29 of his 112 Yorkshire centuries to come.

Sutcliffe's consistency and reliability represented a wonder of cricket right through his most entertaining career. For 21 seasons his lowest aggregate in Yorkshire matches alone was 1,235, and in all matches he scored over 3,000 runs in 1928, 1931 and 1932. In the 8 successive seasons from 1925 to 1932 his average never fell below 50, and in the wet summer of 1931 he made 3,006 runs at an average of 96.96. Throughout his career, it seemed, Sutcliffe had only to be given an assignment to accomplish it.

Wisden has placed it on record as follows:

100 in 1 hour 45 minutes
200 in 3 hours 20 minutes
300 in 4 hours 35 minutes
400 in 5 hours 25 minutes
500 in 6 hours 55 minutes
555 in 7 hours 25 minutes

It was incorrect to believe that this controversial incident did not affect Charlie. In fact, he found the whole situation rather embarrassing. He had to encounter numerous attacks from those in the northern counties, and this hostility grieved him terribly.

Another matter he had to face was the move away from Leyton. After the financial crisis of 1924 games were increasingly played away from the East London town. Colchester, Southend-on-Sea and Chelmsford were already venues, whilst Westcliff-on-Sea, Clacton, and even Brentwood were soon added to the list. 'The Essex Circus', complete with its own travelling scoreboard and other essential equipment travelled from club ground to club ground giving the county a 'true community spirit', with the paying members being made to feel a part of it.

At the end of 1933 Leyton was officially closed as the headquarters of Essex CCC, a move which many players, past and present, regarded very much as a regret. The wickets favoured the batsmen and the ground had neither charm nor beauty, and on a cheerless day it could be quite miserable; yet it had its own character, and many good matches had been played there.

It was Charlie's ground, Percy Perrin's and the ground of Johnny Douglas, now so sadly gone. It was the scene of many incidents, happy and sad, and many great names had trodden the green turf. Its demise was not seen by all as a happy event!

Charlie was, of course, present as scorer at the last game played at Leyton before the ground was sold to the Metropolitan Police. The match was against Somerset on 6 September 1933. He was one of a dwindling band of men left over from the heady 1890s. Neither George Bull, Henry Pickett, Hugh Owen nor Alfred Lucas were there; but Charles Kortright, Percy Perrin and Walter Mead were assembled to enjoy the match with pride.

A fitting tribute was paid to Leyton after the match by Raymond Robertson-Glasgow. He says:

> Many came just to see the game, some I fancy to pay tribute to Essex, not only the triumphant renascent Essex of this year with their youth and fire and ambition, but to the Essex that played at Leyton for nearly half a century that has given in her, great names to cricket . . . . They are deserting the fields of Leyton but they will take with them their memories. The spirit of the many deeds which have enriched their fields . . . . some of those were there to watch this last match on the old, very beloved ground.

Charlie certainly had his memories. The ground, its pavilion and its people had been his life, and a small part of him died that September day. The years had flashed past and his partnerships with Perrin, in the days when Charles Kortright frightened the daylights out of their opponents, seemed an eternity ago!

Those were the days, though; when Essex saw a packed house; when Leyton entertained the fragile Ranji and the grotesque Grace; and when legends such as Victor Trumper and Clem Hill honoured Leyton with their presence. Life would never quite be the same again for Charlie.

How was Charlie to adapt to this move? As a small compensation for East London supporters Ilford was given a week's spot on the schedule of visiting places in Essex. Of course, this was no compensation for Charlie. The move, to him, meant more travelling, something Charlie did not entirely relish.

Journeys to away games were tiresome enough, but now he had to endure the gruelling business of travelling around the county, and at nearly sixty-three years of age he did not want further aggravation. He hardly showed his displeasure, it seems, and by all accounts was as adaptable as ever. A feature, which, according to Tom Cable, only 'added to his charm!'

Travel in the 1930s was mainly undertaken by railway. The journey could be long and arduous and, to relieve the boredom of a monotonous few hours, games of cards were often chosen as forms of entertainment. Tom Pearce recalls: 'Charlie was not backward in joining the card schools set up by the Essex players, and kept the younger men entertained with his humorous stories, usually recounted in cockney rhyming slang.'

Essex was also taking to the road in the 1930s. According to H.D. 'Hopper' Read, journeys to Bristol, Birmingham and Northampton were often attempted by car, if there were enough available.

This was another new experience for Charlie. The roads would have been less congested than nowadays, and it must have been a relaxing and highly enjoyable form of journeying from one place to another. Times had definitely changed since Charlie's playing days when the steam train was the only alternative to the tram or the taxi-cab.

Cricket was a 7 day-a-week occupation for the professional of the 1930s. Even though there was no one-day cricket, most Sundays were spent playing benefit and charity matches. There were more championship matches played, and the club would reimburse rail fares and hotel expenses for the amateur player.

The professional, on the other hand, received an overall allowance and made his own hotel and meal arrangements. Very often players would stay with friends to save them money.

Charlie, always the amateur as a player, by now came into the ranks of the professional. Although not a player, he was employed by the club, and was not in a position to live a life of luxury.

Under the joint captaincy of Tom Pearce, by now an established batsman, and D.R. Wilcox, Essex managed fourth position in 1933. It was consolation for the loss of Leyton and gave Charlie some sort of satisfaction. Essex had not finished higher in the table since 1897, when Charlie had played such a great role 'playing his heart out to the full'.

It is no wonder that Essex performed in such great spirit. They had a formidable pace attack with John Stephenson, Ken Farnes, Stan Nichols, a very young Ray Smith and Hopper Read. It is said of Stephenson that he received or bowled every ball as if his life depended on it, whilst the broad-shouldered, 6ft 5 ins Farnes, was very fast indeed. Hopper Read was a 'match winner' on his day; fiercely fast, he would sacrifice accuracy for speed, whilst Ray Smith was good support as a fast-medium bowler.

1934, however, saw Essex slump to eighth position. They had to adapt to life away from Leyton, with all the wickets completely unknown quantities. Tom Pearce believed the wickets were 'generally better and certainly faster than those prepared today', but the outfield was often rough and bare of grass which added to their problems. Jack O'Connor did manage to score 2,308 runs this season – Jimmy Cutmore, Stan Nichols and Dudley Pope all topped the 1,000 run mark, so the year was not without significance.

13

The Final Journey

The Essex side had the capability, on its day, to beat any team. This was shown convincingly in 1935. Matched against Yorkshire Essex turned the tables on the northern side, after being on the receiving end of Yorkshire's 555 record opening stand three years before. Essex scuttled them out for a meagre 31 runs at Huddersfield and won by an innings and 204 runs.

There is a tale that is told of the Yorkshire committee man who arrived late on the first day and confidently asked the gateman the score. '39 for 9', he was told by the dead-pan official. '39 for 9', replied the committee member, rubbing his hands. 'Champion! Champion! How many wickets has Bowes got?' 'Bowes!' came the incredulous reply, 'bloody Bowes is batting.'

How pleased Essex must have been! It must have gone someway to restore their hurt pride. But this sweet revenge was marred by one sad event. Charlie McGahey was not there to share this historic moment. He was not to experience another World War, nor to feel the sorrow and loss felt by the tragic taking of the handsome Ken Farnes and the likeable Laurie Eastman. Sadly he departed this life in the previous winter, and it was still taking the Essex side, its supporters and Charlie's numerous friends time to adjust to this stunning fact.

On 10 January 1935, a day when *The Times* carried pictures of England's victory over the West Indies in Barbados, Charlie died. He had been at Whipps Cross Hospital, Leytonstone, since the previous Xmas Day and, according to the Coroner's Report – septicaemia had set in following an injury to the little finger of his right-hand due to a fall by kicking against the kerb in the road. A case of accidental death was recorded.

In this day and age it seems inconceivable that someone could die from the effects of a cut finger, but in the mid-1930s medical science was not as it is today. Also, his chances of survival were greatly hindered by the fact that he was somewhat under-nourished. Tom Pearce was quick to raise this point and adds, 'Charlie tended to skip meals in order to make ends meet and so was not fit enough to fight off an infection of that kind.'

Also, his weak chest could not have helped matters. It must have been a great strain on him to stand for long hours, in all conditions, on the playing fields of England. When one considers the state of his health in his early days he, possibly, did well to reach the autumn of his life.

He is buried in West Ham cemetery, which is situated in a quiet area of Forest Gate, off the main shopping area. The burial ground is enclosed with shrubbery, and trees provide a most tranquil setting. It brought Charlie back to his early roots near to Wanstead Flats, where he first found his two great sporting loves.

Clapton Football Club was quite near, and the Liverpool Street to Southend Victoria railway line was away in the distance. The sound of the train, first steam, and later electric, was ever constant, to remind him of far off places. No doubt, Charlie would have preferred to have been laid to rest in his beloved Leyton but, as it happened, he had no such say in the matter. He did not leave a will, nor did he leave enough money for the funeral.

It was left to brother Sydney to make the funeral arrangements and deal with all the necessary costs. Over seventy years of age, Sydney had been widowed since 1921, when his wife Alice died following an operation to remove a cancerous growth. He had purchased a grave on Alice's death capable of holding 3 persons, so when Charlie died, Sydney decided Charlie should be buried next to Alice.

The funeral took place on Tuesday 15 January and a host of celebrities and friends joined Sydney at the graveside to say their farewells. Charles Kortright, Walter Mead, Jack Russell and dear old Bill Reeves, for once solemn in grief, were all there. The many tributes included those from Leyton Football Club, Essex CCC, Leyton Conservative Club and 'Leyton Friends'. Tom Cable recalls that 'Charlie would have abhorred the fuss made', but it was inevitable that his many friends would want to mourn this witty, charming character who gave so much to so many.

This towering man was cheerful and carefree to the end. This

10.   *McGahey turning his arm over.*

showed in a leg-pulling incident recorded in the *Essex Year Book*. A jovial gent kidded with Charlie and brought up the question of the erratic Essex scoreboard. 'Well, would you like to take on the job?' joked Charlie. 'Certainly, if you pay £5 for the match.' 'Impossible!' came the immediate reply from Charlie, 'I doubt if the gate would amount to that and I don't think a collection on the ground would help.'

Poor Charlie only lived for the day and he was always hoping something would turn up to help him earn his crust of bread. He was certainly lucky that Sydney was there to provide for his demise. As it happened Sydney was not so fortunate, and did not obtain his dying wish to be buried with his wife.

Sydney's loyal housekeeper, Amelia Potter, who had tended him so efficiently since Alice's death, died six months after Charlie. He was quite distraught. As she did not leave a family this elderly man had to bury her. The only place was the plot he had bought in West Ham cemetery. He knew, by doing this, he could not be buried there himself, but he felt compelled to take care of her.

Sydney was to live another eight years, finishing his days in Bournemouth, on the Hampshire coast, where a niece of his wife cared for him. The years had taken their toll of his finances, and he left only a few pounds in his will. A sad tale indeed!

Generosity was his downfall, as it was for Charlie, but it must be said Sydney extended his generosity to his family and did not make them an exception as Charlie seemed to do. Sydney and the family were well used to coming to Charlie's assistance and helping him when in need. In Charlie's youth, and into old age he was always the elegant, polished gent who, as far as possible, tried to keep up appearances. The fine suit, the neat shoes and the costly entertainment all added to the budget, and Tom Cable insists his family had to bail him out of many financial scrapes.

I have been unable to ascertain fully how Charlie managed to live the life of a gentleman. He was paid a good sum as Assistant Secretary as has been mentioned, and it is possible that one, or both grandfathers left him some money in his youth. Mrs Swanton was of the opinion that Charlie had money at some time in his life, but in his declining years he was more than grateful to the wages paid to him as coach, and later scorer, to keep the wolf from the door.

A glass of Bass was a great comfort to him. Unlike many other people he was never aggressive nor despondent after its' use. Tom Cable maintained that he never saw Charlie drunk nor worse-for-wear. Even if Charlie did like his Bass he could take it with dignity.

The fact that he did drink was another factor that worried his family. They were, it seems, tea-total, which was a world away from their 'black sheep'. Drink was possibly responsible for the erratic scoreboard in the Yorkshire match of 1932 on Leyton's soil. It was certainly a contributory factor to his fatality. If his mind had been clearer, and more alert it is unlikely he would have stumbled in the manner he did. Being a sociable creature, involved in sport, he would have been indoctrinated at a very early age, as most soccer players and cricketers like nothing better than to partake in a beer, and chat about the game in congenial surroundings. Obviously, this was what he was engaged upon on that fateful Xmas Day in 1934.

Another great comfort to him was knowing that he was considered to be the chief consoler to the Essex team. He would always come to the fore if the side suffered a heavy defeat. According to Charles Bray it was at these precise moments that Charlie would appear in the dressing-room, or railway carriage and relate in his sweet pleasant voice experiences that would make one forget the worries of the day. Bray recalls:

> It will be a lasting regret to me that I never knew him in his prime nor for that matter saw him play cricket. I shall never forget, however, his stories of Grace, Hirst, Rhodes, of Richardson, Buckenham, Douglas and of many other cricket giants of his day. He knew what it was like to be poor in the autumn of his life. It may have been his own fault but never did I know him to be bitter or complaining. He was a most lovable person.!

E.H.D. Sewell went so far as to say 'Charlie was loved by everybody who knew him'. He continues: 'It was indeed a dull day when Charlie Mac. did not make us laugh, for he was full of quips and dry sayings – a man who never made an enemy.'

These words were, of course, echoed by many folk in 1935 when they felt the bitter blow of his loss. Schoolboys missed him terribly, as Charlie was always on hand to pass their autograph books to visiting players, whilst Mrs Swanton and her younger brother would miss the kind man who called on a Sunday and always managed to spare the time for a romp and a play.

The burly figure would no longer be seen on the streets of Leyton, nor at Leyton Football Club in his familiar role selling tickets to the club's many loyal supporters. They could only reminisce how they were privileged to know one of the tallest men in the amateur game. If he had not hailed as such a good cricketer his footballing prowess could not have gone amiss. Even now he is one of only three county cricketers ever to have played soccer for Millwall.

But it is as a cricketer that he is best remembered. In his 685 innings for Essex he made over 19,000 runs and was not out no less than 61 times, and it must be remembered he was also a very useful change bowler.

Charlie first began to bowl on Wanstead Flats, but, in his own estimation, he was 'not very good at it'. This may have been because as Charlie insists: 'I did not try my arm at it until two men were very firmly set, and then if I were not an immediate success tended to be taken off.'

He admitted in *Cricket* in 1896 that 'although I may not as yet have taken a wicket in first-class cricket I have not been punished very severely either.'

Though, when Charlie was pitched against the might of the prolific little run-getter Bobby Abel in a Surrey match in 1895 he really thought he had his first wicket. When Abel was on 199 Charlie bowled to him and thought he had him caught at the wicket. What a prize to take! Unfortunately, the umpire did not think so. Charlie would not have denied him his 200, but declared impishly that 'I could have seen him out off my bowling at 199 without a pang.'

Charlie probably thought his time for revenge was due. The year before he had dropped Abel when the Surrey professional was on 60. It was, supposedly, the easiest catch imaginable. Charlie was no doubt mad with himself and could not understand why the ball would not stay in his hands.

He had to wait a few years for his revenge, but it did come. By

1902 Abel feared Charlie as 'one of the deadliest leg-break bowlers in the business'. Charlie certainly gave him a few worries. The Essex bowler bowled him for 150 and 0 in the Surrey fixture at Leyton with, according to Jephson, 'the variant ball that either went straight or did an inch or two from the off.'

David Frith paid Charlie a very great compliment in his book *The Slow Men*. He compares his system of bowling to that of 'the gargantuan Australian Warwick Armstrong who lured 87 Test batsmen to destruction, much of it self-induced'. As Frith points out: 'Armstrong had a smooth and steady approach and a high delivery.'

Armstrong's real strength was that he would use variation of flight and accuracy of length. He would bowl his leg-breaks for hours if need be, often to a packed leg-side field.

Like Armstrong, Charlie brought the ball down from a great height, enabled it to turn a little in a reliable direction, and was renowned for having every single fieldsmen on the leg-side.

On a crumbling wicket Charlie was feared; as D.L. Jephson described in *Wisden*: 'On a good wicket I would put Charlie McGahey in the potential class – on a broken or crumbling one he is almost at the head of the list.'

Frith claims that 'on one occasion so sporting was his captain A.P. Lucas that he took the demon fast bowler Kortright off when he saw the rough marks he was making in his follow through. McGahey could land on them as if manipulated by a computer, and such tactics offended the sense of decency then prevailing.'

By 1901, Charlie had not only improved enough as a change bowler to gain a place on the 1901-02 to Australia and to be given some credibility by WG, but he also warranted mention in several bibliographies. P.C. Standing was much impressed by the Leyton lad, and rated him as one of the leading bowlers to watch out for in the future.

This he mentioned in a Chapter on *Bowlers of Tomorrow* in his book *Cricket of Today & Yesterday*, written in 1902. Standing says:

> The three bowlers that one can think of at the moment amongst leading English cricketers are perhaps, Mr McGahey, Mr A.O. Jones and W.G. Quaife. The fact is that these three bowlers possess that peculiar quality and 'swerve in the air' which is at all times liable to puzzle and alarm the most

wary and cautious of batsmen, and a fatal facility for changing the pace and regulating the spin which frequently proves fatal indeed to the batsman.

Charlie would have been fun to watch because one would not know whether he would get a wicket or serve up an easy ball for the batsman to knock for 6. Conditions possibly helped him, and may have been instrumental in making him look a better bowler. Perrin said of him: 'He was a very useful change bowler who got us out of many a difficulty. Often perhaps, a bowler such as himself would get a wicket after Kortright, Mead or Bull had toiled all day to no avail.'

Sewell felt Charlie took wickets by 'downright fraud'. He thought Charlie's pretence at bowling leg-breaks was really shameless, but added that 'here and there wickets fell'.

The Cricketer, though, in Charlie's obituary, believed Charlie to be a 'much better slow bowler than many people thought, having a flight which was decidedly deceptive.' The Middlesex batsman, W.P. Robertson, certainly found him a problem. Robertson disliked Charlie's bowling intensely, and used to exclaim to his partner: 'I know McGahey's a rotten bowler but for the love of heaven don't let him bowl to me as he always gets me out.' This was absolutely true, much to Robertson's disgust, and Charlie's amusement.

No doubt Charlie found bowling a great challenge, especially if he was up against batsmen such as Robertson. He naturally had a psychological advantage over a batsman who feared him, and by sheer cheek could unnerve his opposition and lure him to his death.

On two occasions he did the 'match double' of 100 runs and 10 wickets. Against Gloucestershire, at Bristol, in 1901, he made scores of 66 and 91 and took 12–157, and in 1906, at Leyton, he had a big share in the first ever win for Essex against Nottinghamshire, scoring 89 and 14, whilst taking 10–64 (7–27 in the first innings).

Charlie persevered. He worked hard to try and improve upon the few skills he had as a bowler because he obviously wanted to contribute to the Essex attack and not be just a good fielder for his county.

His hard work paid off, and he deserved his 'just acclaim',

which occurred at a time when Essex CCC were the Cinderellas of cricket. What would he, and the other Essex faithfuls have thought of today's many achievements?

Essex' playing record since 1979 shows a level of success unmatched by any other county: four county championships, three Sunday titles, one NatWest Trophy and one Benson and Hedges Cup. The modern visitor to Chelmsford cannot fail to be impressed by a neat, well-appointed ground, which is truly a model headquarters for a county club with a membership of around 9,000 and a healthy balance sheet.

He would have been so proud of the team coming to the fore and realizing their full potential, and would certainly not have envied their just acclaim. It is a pity that some of their success did not come during Charlie's lifetime, but alas that was not to be!

He had stayed around long enough to view with his own eyes the great years of Hendren; of Hammond; and he that was 'all summer', Frank Woolley. He had seen the ball made smaller, the stumps increased in height and breadth, and had witnessed Jack Hobbs make the run required to pass W.G. Grace's career record of 34,896 runs.

Charlie gave himself to sport, and was rewarded with a rich and colourful life – never mundane nor lacking in excitement. What was there left for him? He had explored nearly every avenue. Like Leyton, his deed was done; like Leyton he would not be forgotten.

His many friends held him in high esteem and admired his warmth and kindness, being a man devoid of malice and generous to all. But they also realized he squandered his money, and resented the fact that he was compelled to work into old age. A fund was set up for him in the months prior to his death and a cheque was to be presented to him the following summer.

It would have meant Charlie could have enjoyed retirement and been free from the pecuniary worries that had for so long troubled him. A sad end to an eventful life. But then would Charlie have had it any other way? Would he have accepted 'charity', as he would have put it, and could he have accepted complete retirement? I think the answers are *NO*. Perhaps it was better for him to go as he did, rather than sink into oblivion, away from the only life he knew.

Career Statistics – C.P. McGahey

Compiled by Robert Brooke

SEASON-BY-SEASON RECORD

1894—1899 (5-ball overs)

Season	M	Inns	No	Runs	HS	Ave	100	50	Ct	Overs	Mdns	Runs	Wkts	Ave
1894	5	10	1	91	24	10.11	–	–	1	2	0	8	0	
1895	16	31	3	702	147	25.07	1	4	6	10	3	38	1	
1896	17	32	1	706	97	22.77	–	4	5	25	7	78	2	39.00
1897	19	33	1	1050	140	32.81	2	6	11	55	15	144	6	24.00
1898	21	33	2	1089	145	35.12	2	5	11	64	15	190	5	38.00
1899	21	35	4	983	130	31.70	1	6	6					
Total	99	174	12	4621	147	28.52	6	25	40	156	40	458	14	32.71

1900-1921

Season	M	Inns	No	Runs	HS	Ave	100	50	Ct	Overs	Mdns	Runs	Wkts	Ave	St	1om
1900	21	34	2	1190	184	37.18	4	2	1	52	8	171	3	57.00	6	
1901	24	43	5	1838	145*	48.36	5	11	11	558	128	1482	52	28.50		2
1901-02	7	12	2	210	57	21.00	–	1	3	61.3	13	165	7	23.57	1	
1902	25	42	6	1240	126	34.44	2	10	12	401.3	92	989	42	23.54		
1903	22	41	5	1144	144*	31.77	2	4	6	149.5	32	400	9	44.44		
1904	24	41	3	1477	225	38.86	3	5	11	317	70	900	29	31.03	1	
1905	26	46	3	1783	277	41.46	3	8	9	212.2	36	671	22	30.50	1	
1906	23	43	2	1217	101	29.68	1	7	9	155	27	423	18	23.50		1
1907	27	46	4	1206	108	28.71	1	7	8	170.4	12	703	26	27.03		
1908	19	29	4	886	230	35.44	2	4	6	204.5	30	687	24	28.62		
1909	19	33	1	719	77	22.46	–	4	4	142.1	18	580	8	72.50		
1910	20	35	6	880	89*	30.34	–	10	3	59.2	13	181	7	25.85		
1911	17	28	5	506	71	22.00	–	2	6	156.3	27	561	12	46.75		
1912	18	29	2	653	150	24.18	2	1	5	175.1	23	687	21	32.71	1	
1913	11	19	0	227	56	11.94	–	1	5	57	7	218	4	54.50		
1914	6	8	0	163	71	20.37	–	2	2	27	5	103	3	34.33		
1919	6	10	0	166	39	16.60	–	–	2	53	3	264	13	20.30	1	
1920	22	36	3	591	66*	17.90	–	2	6	159.5	13	648	16	40.50	1	
1921	1	2	0	6	6	3.00	–	–	1	1	0	9	0			
Total	338	577	53	16102	277	30.73	25	81	110	3113.4	557	9842	316	31.15	12	3
Career Total	437	751	65	20723	277	30.20	31	106	150	3269.4	597	10300	330	31.21	12	3

133

RECORD FOR ESSEX – BY GROUNDS

HOME GROUNDS

Ground	M	Inns	No	Runs	HS	Ave	100	50	Ct	Overs	Mdns	Runs	Wkts	Ave	St	1om	BB
Leyton	195	330	31	10116	277	33.83	18	56	74	58† 1416.3‡	12 269	4556	152	29.97	5	2	7/27
Southend	4	7	0	210	82	30.00	–	1	1	46	6	208	7	29.71	–	–	3/72
Colchester	2	4	0	26	11	6.50	–	–	1	19	1	82	0		–	–	
Total	201	341	31	10352	277	33.39	18	57	76	58† 1481.3‡	12 276	4846	159	30.47	5	2	7/27

AWAY GROUNDS

Ground	M	Inns	No	Runs	HS	Ave	100	50	Ct	Overs	Mdns	Runs	Wkts	Ave	St	1om	BB
Derby	15	25	4	776	115	36.95	1	5	5	26† 48.5‡	8 9	208	12	17.33	1	–	5/24
Chesterfield	2	3	0	105	68	35.00	–	1	1	35	7	97	0		–	–	
Glossop	2	4	0	148	73	37.00	–	1	–	14	7	29	5	5.80	–	–	3/8
Clifton	4	7	0	262	91	37.42	–	2	2	4† 77‡	1 15	197	15	13.13	2	1	6/71
Bristol	3	4	0	37	17	9.25	–	–	1	26	1	120	3	40.00	–	–	2/56
Cheltenham	1	2	0	20	15	10.00	–	–	1	4	0	36	0		–	–	
Southampton	8	14	2	329	67	27.41	–	3	1	1	1	0	0		–	–	
Bournemouth	3	6	0	132	57	22.00	–	1	–	15	1	76	2	38.00	–	–	1/19
Portsmouth	1	2	0	40	22	20.00	–	–	–	18	3	56	1		–	–	1/56
Canterbury	5	9	0	232	95	25.77	–	2	2	96.3	22	287	10	28.70	1	–	6/95
Tonbridge	3	6	1	118	45*	23.60	–	–	2	15	1	56	2	28.00	–	–	1/23
Gravesend	2	4	0	14	14	3.50	–	–	2	8	1	33	2	16.50	–	–	2/12
Tunbridge Wells	2	3	0	228	108	76.00	2	–	3	20	2	80	2	40.00	–	–	1/23
Dover	1	2	0	2	2	1.00	–	–	–	3	0	28	0		–	–	
Maidstone	1	2	0	22	18	11.00	–	–									
Old Trafford	14	25	2	733	145	31.86	2	2	3	64	8	177	5	35.40	–	–	3/30
Liverpool	3	5	0	81	43	16.20	–	–	–	4	0	29	0		–	–	
Leicester:																	
Aylestone Road	10	17	2	631	99	42.06	–	6	2	6† 72‡	0 17	221	8	27.62	–	–	4/68
Grace Road	5	8	0	392	123	49.00	1	3	2	6†	3	15	0		–	–	

CAREER STATISTICS

Ground	M	I	NO	Runs	HS	Avge	100	50	Ct	Overs	Mdns	Runs	Wkts	Avge	5i	10m	Best
Lord's	18	32	3	645	137	22.24	1	1	9	1† / 135.3‡	0 / 25	498	8	62.25	–	–	2/9
Northampton	7	13	2	461	230	41.90	1	3	1	38	6	135	4	33.75	–	–	3/46
Trent Bridge	11	19	3	383	74*	23.93	–	3	1	118	20	323	6	53.83	–	–	2/47
Weston-s-Mare	3	3	0	25	21	8.33	–	–	4	12	1	45	7	6.42	1	–	6/21
Taunton	1	1	0	147	147	–	1	–	2	–	–	–	–	–	–	–	–
The Oval	21	38	4	1020	173	30.00	3	3	5	19† / 154.1‡	5 / 39	554	20	27.70	1	–	5/93
Hove	11	20	3	585	140	34.41	1	3	4	12† / 114.1‡	5 / 21	320	13	24.61	1	–	5/58
Eastbourne	4	7	0	126	45	18.00	–	–	–	35	3	120	2	60.00	–	–	2/77
Hastings	1	2	0	79	58	39.50	–	1	1	31	4	94	2	47.00	–	–	1/25
Horsham	1	–	–	–	–	–	–	–	–	19	0	81	2	40.50	–	–	2/81
Edgbaston	11	20	2	432	77	24.00	–	3	1	12† / 67.3‡	3 / 6	244	8	30.50	–	–	3/68
Worcester	2	2	0	4	4	2.00	–	–	–	20	5	72	2	36.00	–	–	1/7
Bournville	1	1	–	–	–	–	–	–	•	2	0	10	0	–	–	–	–
Stourbridge	1	1	0	21	21	–	–	–	–	3	0	–	0	–	–	–	–
Bradford	5	10	0	97	25	9.70	–	–	1	28‡	5	122	1	–	–	–	1/88
Leeds	3	6	0	33	20	5.50	–	–	–	13	2	49	1	–	–	–	1/28
Sheffield	3	4	0	67	55	16.75	–	–	4	15	1	44	1	–	–	–	–
Dewsbury	2	4	1	52	32*	17.33	–	–	–	3	0	14	0	–	–	–	–
Harrogate	2	4	1	86	55*	28.66	–	–	1	–	–	–	–	–	–	–	–
Huddersfield	2	4	0	58	40	14.50	–	–	2	5	0	26	1	–	–	–	1/26
Hull	1	1	0	3	3	–	–	–	1	–	–	–	–	–	–	–	–
Cambridge	2	3	0	50	24	16.66	–	–	1	27	2	86	2	43.00	–	–	1/15
Oxford	1	2	0	51	26	25.50	–	–	–	17	2	53	1	–	–	–	1/47
Total	400	685	61	19079	277	30.57	29	99	139	148† / 2856.1‡	38 / 512	9481	306	30.98	29	12	7/27

* Not out † 5-ball overs ‡ 6-ball overs

RECORD FOR ESSEX – v – EACH OPPONENT

	M	Inns	No	Runs	HS	Ave	100	50	Ct	Overs	Mdns	Runs	Wkts	Ave	St	Iom	BB
Derbyshire	38	63	7	2246	277	40.10	4	13	16	27 † / 263.5‡	8 / 60	836	28	29.85	1	–	5/24
Gloucs	17	29	1	963	145*	34.39	3	4	4	16 † / 166 ‡	2 / 27	615	21	29.28	2	1	6/71
Hampshire	20	34	3	828	87	26.70	–	7	3	4 / 47	1 / 4	186	3	62.00	–	–	1/19
Kent	30	52	4	1368	142	28.50	3	6	14	14 † / 212.3‡	3 / 38	769	27	28.48	2	–	6/56
Lancashire	36	61	6	1638	145	29.78	2	8	11	176.5	24	583	13	44.84	–	–	3/29
Leics	29	49	6	1754	184	40.79	2	14	6	12 † / 135.4‡	3 / 33	379	17	22.29	–	–	4/68
Middlesex	29	52	3	1342	137	27.38	3	4	11	278.5	52	938	19	49.36	–	–	2/9
Northants	12	21	2	620	230	32.63	1	2	2	86	7	321	11	29.18	–	–	3/46
Notts	22	37	5	1041	225	32.53	1	7	6	342.4	62	983	42	23.40	2	2	7/27
Somerset	5	6	0	237	147	39.50	1	1	7	12	1	45	7	6.42	1	–	6/21
Surrey	41	76	9	1981	173	29.56	2	9	16	22 † / 354 ‡	5 / 89	1143	43	26.58	1	–	5/93
Sussex	34	53	5	1701	140	35.43	4	9	9	12 † / 337.2‡	5 / 52	1097	34	32.26	2	–	5/58
Warwicks	23	40	4	1126	130	31.27	2	5	7	37 † / 137.5‡	11 / 17	518	22	23.54	1	–	5/95
Worcs	7	8	2	201	66*	33.50	–	2	2	28	5	104	2	52.00	–	–	1/7
Yorkshire	36	66	2	1077	105	16.82	1	4	17	3 † / 128.4‡	0 / 21	444	7	63.42	–	–	2/12

MCC	3	5	0	67	20	13.40	–	–	3	1	0	8	0	–	–	–	–
Cambridge Univ.	2	3	0	50	24	16.66	–	–	1	27	2	86	2	43.00	–	–	1/15
Oxford Univ.	1	2	0	51	26	25.50	–	–	–	17	2	53	1	–	–	–	1/47
Australians	11	20	2	599	72	33.27	–	3	4	75	14	280	3	93.33	–	–	2/59
West Indians	1	2	0	108	82	54.00	–	1	–	9	1	23	0	–	–	–	–
South Africans	3	6	0	81	43	13.50	–	–	–	21	1	70	4	17.50	–	–	2/10
Total	400	685	61	19079	277	30.57	29	99	139	148 †	38	9481	306	30.98	12	3	7/27
										2856.1 ‡	512						

RECORD FOR OTHER TEAMS IN ENGLAND

	M	Ins	No	Runs	HS	Ave	100	50	Ct	Overs	Mdns	Runs	Wkts	Ave	St	1om	BB
Gentlemen	9	18	1	423	68	24.88	–	3	3	8† 28‡	2 6	104	1	–	–	–	1/37
London County	7	10	1	559	102*	62.11	2	2	3	124	22	355	10	35.50	–	–	4/17
Gents of South	3	5	0	74	30	14.80	–	–	–	12	2	37	0	–	–	–	–
South	3	6	0	120	45	20.00	–	–	–								
Bamford's XI	1	2	0	13	9	6.50	–	–	1	7	0	42	2	21.00	–	–	2/42
De la Warrs XI	1	2	0	18	18	9.00	–	1	–								
East	1	2	0	76	59	38.00	–	1	–	1	0	2	0	–	–	–	–
England XI	1	1	0	24	24	–	–	–	–	16	1	96	2	48.00	–	–	1/36
WG Grace's XI	1	2	0	11	9	5.50	–	–	–								
MCC	1	2	0	69	35	34.50	–	–	–								
The Rest	1	2	0	43	43	21.50	–	–	1	8	1	18	2	9.00	–	–	2/18
Wembley Park	1	2	0	4	4	2.00	–	–	–								
Total	30	54	2	1434	102*	27.57	2	6	8	8† 196‡	2 32	654	17	38.47	–	–	4/17

GROUND RECORDS FOR ALL TEAMS PLAYED FOR IN ENGLAND

	M	Ins	No	Runs	HS	Ave	100	50	Ct	Overs	Mdns	Runs	Wkts	Ave	St	1om	BB
The Oval	31	58	5	1470	173	27.73	1	5	9	27† 187.1‡	7 47	661	21	31.47	1	–	5/93
Hastings	5	9	0	194	58	21.55	–	1	1	46	5	136	4	34.00	–	–	2/18
Bournemouth	4	8	0	187	57	23.37	–	1	–	20	3	89	2	44.50	–	–	1/19
Chesterfield	3	5	0	171	68	34.20	–	1	1	45	7	131	0	–	–	–	–
Lord's	19	34	3	714	137	23.03	1	1	9	1† 135.3‡	0 25	498	8	62.25	–	–	2/9
Oxford	2	4	0	114	51	28.50	–	1	–	18	2	57	1	–	–	–	1/47

RECORD ON EACH GROUND FOR OTHER TEAMS IN ENGLAND

	M	Inns	No	Runs	HS	Ave	100	50	Ct	Overs	Mdns	Runs	Wkts	Ave	St	Iom	BB
The Oval	10	20	1	450	68	23.68	–	2	4	8†/33‡	2/8	107	1	–	–	–	1/37
Crystal Palace	5	6	1	414	115	82.80	2	2	2	108	20	314	10	31.40	–	–	4/17
Hastings	4	7	0	115	45	16.42	–	–	1	15	1	42	2	21.00	–	–	2/18
Blackpool	2	3	0	90	39	30.00	–	–	–	16	1	96	2	48.00	–	–	1/36
Bexhill	1	2	0	18	18	9.00	–	–	1								
Bournemouth	1	2	0	55	30	27.50	–	–	–	5	2	13	0				
Cardiff	1	2	0	76	59	38.00	–	1	–	1	0	2	0				
Chesterfield	1	2	0	66	44	33.00	–	–	–	10	0	34	0				
Lord's	1	2	0	69	35	34.50	–	1	–								
Oxford	1	2	0	63	51	31.50	–	1	–	1	0	4	0				
Scarborough	1	2	0	1	1	0.50	–	–	–								
Uttoxeter	1	2	0	13	9	6.50	–	–	–	7	0	42	2	21.00	–	–	2/42
Wembley Park	1	2	0	4	4	2.00	–	–	–								
Total	30	54	2	1434	115	27.57	2	6	8	8†/196‡/32	2/32	654	17	38.47	–	–	4/17

139

RECORD FOR MCC IN AUSTRALIA 1901–02

	M	Inns	No	Runs	HS	Ave	100	50	Ct	Overs	Mdns	Runs	Wkts	Ave	St	1om	BB
TEST MATCHES																	
Sydney	1	2	0	31	18	15.50	–	–	–								
Melbourne	1	2	0	7	7	3.50	–	–	1								
Total	2	4	0	38	18	9.50	–	–	1								
MATCHES AGAINST OTHER TEAMS																	
Victoria	2	4	1	110	57	36.66	–	1	–	17.4	0	71	5	14.20	–	–	3/58
New South Wales	2	3	1	41	32*	20.50	–	–	1	26	10	59	0	–	–	–	–
South Australia	1	1	0	21	21	–	–	–	1	17.5	3	35	2	17.50	–	–	2/35
Full Total	7	12	2	210	57	21.00	–	1	3	61.3	13	165	7	23.57	–	–	3/58
GROUND RECORDS IN AUSTRALIA																	
Melbourne	3	6	1	117	57	23.40	–	1	1	17.4	0	71	5	14.20	–	–	3/58
Sydney	3	5	1	72	32*	18.00	–	–	1	26	10	59	0	–	–	–	–
Adelaide	1	1	0	21	21	–	–	–	1	17.5	3	35	2	17.50	–	–	2/35
Total	7	12	2	210	57	21.00	–	1	3	61.3	13	165	7	23.57	–	–	3/58

DOUBLE CENTURIES IN FIRST-CLASS CRICKET

277	Essex v Derbyshire, Leyton	1905
230	Essex v Northamptonshire, Northampton	1908
225	Essex v Nottinghamshire, Leyton	1904

BEST BOWLING ANALYSES IN FIRST-CLASS CRICKET

7–27	Essex v Nottinghamshire, Leyton	1906
6–21	Essex v Somerset, Weston-super-mare	1919

BEST MATCH ANALYSES IN FIRST-CLASS CRICKET

12–157	Essex v Gloucestershire, Clifton	1901
10–64	Essex v Nottinghamshire, Leyton	1906

MATCH DOUBLES

66 & 91; 6-86 & 6-71; Essex v Gloucestershire, Clifton		1901
89 & 14; 7-27 & 3-37; Essex v Nottinghamshire, Leyton		1906

McGahey's highest score in any grade of cricket is believed to be 305* for an Essex XI v Carmarthenshire at Llanelli, 9–10 July 1906.

Bibliography

SOCIAL HISTORY

Charles Booth:	*Late-Victorian Social Survey of London*
Janet & Peter Philips:	*Victorians at Home & Away*
Donald Read:	*England 1868–1914 – The Age of Urban Democracy*
L.C.B. Seaman:	*Life in Victorian London*
Nerina Shute:	*More London Villages*
Edward Walford:	*Village London – The story of Greater London*

SOCCER

Bob Barton:	*Non-League: A History of League & Cup Football*
Bob Barton:	*Servowarm History of the FA Amateur Cup*
C.W. Alcock & Rowland Hill:	*Famous Footballers*
H. Long:	*Clapton FC's First 50 Years*
Philip Soar:	*The Spurs Go Marching On*

CRICKET

Trevor Bailey:	*A History of Cricket*
Charles Bray:	*Essex County Cricket*
Gerald Brodribb:	*The Croucher*
Lionel H. Brown:	*Victor Trumper & The 1902 Australians*
D.K. Darling:	*Test Tussles on and off the field*
David Frith:	*The Slow Men*
David Kynaston:	*Bobby Abel – Professional Batsman*
David Lemmon:	*Johnny Won't Hit Today*
Christopher Martin-Jenkins:	*Cricket – A Way of Life*
	Wisden Book of County Cricket
F.R.D.O. Monro:	*Repton Cricket (1901-1951)*
P. Morrah:	*The Golden Age of Cricket*
Raymond Robertson-Glasgow:	*46 Not Out*
Charles Sale:	*Korty, The Legend Explained*
E.H.D. Sewell:	*Cricket & How to Play it*
	An Outdoor Wallah
P.C. Standing:	*Cricket of Today & Yesterday*

Philip Thorn, Philip Bailey,
   Peter Wynne-Thomas: *Who's Who of Cricketers*
James Thorpe: *Cricket in a Bag*
P. Warner: *Gents & Players 1806–1949*

NEWSPAPERS & PERIODICALS

*Sportfolio Portraits & Biographies of Heroes & Heroines
   – Sport & Pastimes*
Men Famous in Football
The Leytonstone Express & Independent
Cricket
The Times
The Daily Express
Essex Year Books
Wisden Cricketers Almanack
Cricketer

Index

145

List of Subscribers

The author has been greatly encouraged by the level of interest in this book, particularly from the under-mentioned who placed orders in advance of publication.

I A Ackroyd
A C Agent
M B Alexander
Don Ambrose
R J Amor
Edgar L Appleby
Jonathan P Atkinson
R N Axten
H S Barr-Hamilton
A Beecroft
M A Beer
Andrew Birch
John J Blackmore
David Boorman
Michael A Brennan
G T Brewster
D F Bull
D F Carruthers
Mervyn Carson FCCA AITI
M J Chandler
R M Charlesworth
R B Charlton
P R Clausen-Thue
G A Copinger
B Corke
Brian A C Croudy
G P E Curry
Alan Davies

Stephen De Winton
Tony Debenham
Tony Dey
C D N Dickman
Donal H Donovan
David Edney
S R Eley
N F S Epps
John Ferguson
Paul A Filer
Gerald W Fisher
Neil Fowler
Charles Fox
John Gallimore
H D Garrod
Michael Gerken
Frank Grant
Ray L Greenall
H J W Gunton
Andrew Hardy
David Hardy
Brian Heald
Kevin Henriques
B E Herman
Dr A K Hignell
J J Hooton
W F Hopkins
A M Hoskins

151

K R Hounsome
David A Jeater
L W Jenkinson
Neil Jenkinson
John Jewitt
Roy A Johnstone
P L Jones
L S Kale
D A Lambert
D R Lee
John Leonard
W H Howard Lewis
Steven Lynch
S R Mair
Andrew W J Makinson
David S Marsh
R M Marshall
J F Mendl
Michael J Metson
A D Mitchener
S D Nead
Michael Oliver
Raymond Owen
Roger Packham
M L Pearce
M R Pearce
Sally Pearce
Stephen Pickles
Andy Porter
Rev G Alex Potts
William A Powell
David Pracy
Charles W Price
David Rayvern Allen
John E Reeves
A O Renny
D P Reynolds
S E Rickard
E M Ring

R C Robinson
Michael P Ronayne
K J Rosewell
C P Rothwell
J F S Russell
S H Sharpley
Tony Sheldon
P R Sheppard
Roderick Smith
J G Spencer
D J Sperring
M C Spurrier
Peter J Stanley
C Stephens
G D Stephens MBE
Herbert Stephenson
Maria Stocker
Dave Sullivan
D I G Tait
Donald J W Taylor
M G Taylor
Mervyn Thomas
M D Thompson
John A Townsend
Richard Turbet
L W Varossieau
A C Viney
Keith Walmsley
Kenneth R Watkin
D G Wayte
Michael Webb
Professor G Derek West
Marcus K Williams
C J Wilson
Robby Wilton
Anthony Woodhouse
Richard Woods
L A Woolcott